THE POLITICS OF REGIONALISM IN SOUTH ASIA

B. MOHANAN

ATLANTIC PUBLISHERS & DISTRIBUTORS

Published by
ATLANTIC PUBLISHERS AND DISTRIBUTORS
B-2, Vishal Enclave, New Delhi - 27
Phone: 5413460

Sales office
4215/1, Ansari Road, Darya Ganj
New Delhi - 110002
Phone : 3273880

Typeset at
APD Computer Graphics
B-2, Vishal Enclave, N. Delhi - 27

Printed in india at
Mehra Offset Press
New Delhi

FOREWORD

The hallmark of contemporary international politics is the proliferation of regional groupings of varied nature and scope. The proclivity in the post-Second World War period has been towards several worlds instead of one. This was generally the trend even in the various conferences held during the course of the Second World War. The powers that participated in these conferences agreed that the new organisation should be given unquestionable authority to deal with issues of war and peace. But at the same time they reiterated the importance of regionalism that might play a positive role in the settlement of local disputes.

The Euro-centric international system paled into insignificance after the Second World War. The process of decolonisation resulted in the emergence of a large number of states in Asia and Africa. These newly independent countries found the regional framework, co-operation and integration to be the most suitable strategy of development. It is being widely accepted as a strategy for meeting the challenges of the present unjust world economic order and overcoming internal structural inadequacies.

In fact the increasing tendency for South-South Co-operation is one of the essential components of the New International Economic Order. International trade flow is today dominated by the 'North'. South-South co-operation is perhaps the only way out to counter the growing trend of protectionism practised by the developed countries. Collective self-reliance will boost the morale of the states in the South and increase their bargaining power. The motivating factors behind regional co-operation are power, influence and security apart from economic factors.

It is against this broad canvas that Mr. Mohanan, a young and up-coming scholar on international relations, examines the formation of SAARC and the problems of regional co-operation in South Asia.

Regional co-operation among South Asian nations was institutionalised with the formation of SAARC at Dhaka on 8 December 1985. The salient features of the Dhaka Declaration and the Charter adopted on 8 December were that the Heads of States of seven countries realised that SAARC would play an important role in accelerating the pace of economic and social development, promote material and collective self-reliance and further the cause of peace, progress and stability in South Asia and the world.

After tracing the evolution of SAARC Mr. Mohanan briefly reviews the South Asian experience of regionalism within the broad framework of regional integration theory. Theories of functionalism and neo-functionalism are discussed in this context. The functionalist, neo-functionalist theories of integration are based upon the traditional customs union theory with its famous typology of free trade area, customs union and complete economic-integration. The origins of the economic theory of integration is attributed to Jacob Viner's book 'The Customs Union Issue'. The underlying principle of the theory is comparative advantage and the attainment of increased welfare through the freeing of trade. A relatively high level of political integration is a primary requirement for an integrative scheme aimed at collective self-reliances, he observes. Nationalist pulls and pressures, nature of leadership, domestic political conditions, intra-regional political and economic relations and extra-regional factors play a key role in South Asian regional system.

Based on this theoretical frame of reference, Mr. Mohanan attempts to study the politics of regionalism in South Asia in the remaining chapters of the monograph. The political economy of South Asia is ably presented in Chapter III followed by Chapter IV on 'Regional Co-operation and Development: The South Asian Experience'. This chapter sketches the modalities and mechanisms SAARC as evolved for the purpose of implementing, co-ordinating and monitoring its activities and assesses the progress SAARC has made so far in the agreed upon areas of co-operation. An attempt is made to relate the course of SAARC co-operation to the theme of community formation. A review of the external environment is made followed by an analysis of the ASEAN documents to draw lessons from the ASEAN experiences in this respect. The most important lesson drawn from the ASEAN experience in respect of community formation can be reduced to three key words: informality, frequent consultations and patience. The South Asian fabric of multilateral co-operation is fundamentally different from that of ASEAN. The harmonised external policy of ASEAN is facilitated by the close ideological and political orientation of the ASEAN states. Such a consensus on basic political and ideological values is not available in SAARC region to stabilise and strengthen the sketchy emergence of SAARC solidarity. Intra-regional political issues, tensions and instability are well manipulated by the extra-regional actors in accordance with their global rivalry and competition.

In the concluding chapter Mr. Mohanan makes certain critical remarks which are borne-out by his perceptive analysis of the politico-economic milieu of South Asia. He rightly maintains that SAARC has not yet taken any of the important functional domains for multilateral cooperation. Issues of marginal importance like SAARC Audio Visual Exchange, food security reserve, sports and games have been discussed. SAARC is not at all interested in functional goals of supranationality. It is highly limited in scope and dimensions.

Mr. Mohanan's study is very well-documented. It reveals his ability to collect relevent data, process them scientifically and arrive at logical conclusions. His clarity of thought and ability for perceptive analaysis are well reflected throughout this study. Written in simple and persuasive style, the study will be extremely useful to students of South Asia and Regionalism and is indeed a welcome addition to the scanty literature on regionalism in South Asia. I have great pleasure in recommending this excellent study to the students of international relations as well as to the planners and administrators.

Prof. K. Raman Pillai
Formerly Professor & Head,
Department of Politics,
Dean, Faculty of Social Sciences,
University of Kerala

PREFACE AND ACKNOWLEDGEMENTS

Thanks to the determined efforts of the late Zia-ur-Rahman of Bangladesh, South Asia got a regional forum for multilateral co-operation. People of South Asia and the world at large witnessed five summits of the Association since it was formally launched in 1985 at Dhaka. The Association established its secretariat at Kathmandu and at the Islamabad Summit, "SAARC 2000: A basic needs perspective" was adopted. Even after all these, the "poor man's club" could not enter into the core areas of co-operation owing to bilateral irritants and strategic discord.

This brings home the fact that the federal, plural, functional and neo-functional approaches developed in the context of West European integration would not be feasible in a third world region like that of South Asia. Supranational handling of political and economic issues are not possible in a developing region, where sovereignty is "jealously" guarded. This is not to say that the insights thrown open by David Mitrany, Ernest Hass, Karl Deutsch, J.S. Nye, Bela Balassa and a host of others are totally irrelevant to the study and analysis of regional co-operation in South Asia. A regional framework established for development should have complex institutions and broader range of policies to deal with the political implications of economic co-operation.

Following the formal initiative on South Asian Regional Co-operation, academic Journals, Periodicals and Newspapers came out with study reports and analytical articles about the impediments and constraints, problems and prospects of region building in South Asia. A few books also appeared.

Even a cursory look at the existing literature would bring home the fact that all the existing studies have concentrated on a few themes. Differences in foreign policy perceptions, India's pivotal role, asymmetrical power structure, dependence-dominance syndrome nature of the political system and the question of political will are the themes which received attention. However all these subjects have not been adequately and equally attended. Another important fact that can be noticed is that all the studies represent individual country perspectives. An Indian perspective, a Nepali perspective and so on and so forth. A comprehensive study embracing all the relevant aspects of the phenomenon of South Asian regionalism which represents an integral view has yet to appear.

The existing literature can be classified into two categories, *viz.*, economic-cultural and the political approaches. The economic-cultural approach represents the simple to the difficult way of looking at the process of regionalism. Adherents of this approach believe that co-operation in non-political areas will have a spillover effect upon the political areas. The political perspective or primacy of the political speaks of resolving the outstanding issues first to pave the way for an effective multilateral framework of co-operation. Blending of these two would suit the unique nature of this region and that would be more pragmatic.

Many institutions and individuals helped me in my study. I am grateful to the University Grants Commission for providing a fellowship to carry out the research and to the Indian Council of Social Science Research for providing the travel grant. I gratefully remember the facilities extented to me by the staff of the Kerala University Library, Politics Department Library (Trivandrum), Jawaharlal Nehru University Library (New Delhi), Indian Council of World Affairs Library (New Delhi), Institute of Defence Studies and Analysis Library (New Delhi), Ministry of External Affairs Library (New Delhi), American Centre Library (New Delhi), Documentation Centre, ICSSR (New Delhi), Centre for South and South East Asian Studies, University of Madras and the Diplomatic Missions of the South Asian Countries in New Delhi. I have greatly benefited from the extensive discussions I had with a number of scholars and academics in Trivandrum, Madras and New Delhi. I am particularly grateful to Dr. V. Suryanarayan, Prof. and Head, Centre for South and South East Asian Studies, University of Madras, Dr. S.D. Muni, Professor of South Asian Studies, School of International Studies, Jawaharlal Nehru University, New Delhi and Dr. Manoranjan Mohanthy, Professor of Political Science, University of Delhi.

The idea of working on South Asian regionalism came down to me in the form of suggestions by Dr. Surjit Mansingh, Professor, School of International Service, American University, Washington D.C., in 1981, when she was Visiting Professor, Department of Politics, University of Kerala. I am indebted to this distinguished scholar for putting me on the right track.

I am deeply obliged to Dr. K. Raman Pillai, former Professor and Head of the Department of Politics, University of Kerala for his kind help, encouragement, constructive suggestions and proper guidance of my research all along by his critical comments and observations. Without his help this study might not have been completed.

I must also express my sincere thanks to a number of my friends and well wishers who provided invaluable assistance at different stages of the progress of the study.

B. Mohanan

CONTENTS

CHAPTER I

INTRODUCTION

The constructive idea for regional co-operative framework in South Asia was mooted by the late Zia-ur-Rehman of Bangladesh in 1980. He was pondering over the idea for some time. The President utilised his visits to the South Asian capitals during the second half of the 70s and also his meetings with his counterparts during the Regional Commonwealth Summit (Sidney) and Commonwealth Summit (Havana) for informally sounding them on this idea. In like manner his Foreign Minister also informally discussed the idea with his counterparts during the bitlateral visits and also meetings during the sessions of the UN General Assembly and other international forums.[1] However the idea acquired specific shape when President Zia-ur-Rehman, during his State visit to Sri Lanka, suggested a summit meeting of South Asian countries to launch the association.

It could be seen that he worked hard to create a favourable atmosphere to his proposal.[2] He despatched letters to the heads of state in which he "not only applauded the recent development which had created a better climate of understanding but also underlined the urgency of institutional arrangement."[3]

The President said that "the countries of South Asia share many common values that are rooted in their social, ethnic, cultural and historical traditions. Perceptions about certain specific events or political situation of the world may differ, but such differences do not seem to create a gulf between them that cannot be bridged. In fact, the beginning of co-operation on a regional basis may be a positive force in generating a climate of harmony conducive to a better perception of what the countries in the region have in common and the value of this shared heritage."[4]

It should be mentioned that he presented his argument to suit the standpoint of a small nation. He stated:

In South Asia, as in other regions of the world, we have countries at different levels of development, some are relatively less developed than others. Any proposal for economic co-operation must consequently be formulated with the greatest care in order to ensure that the weak are not exploited and that the strong do not dominate. The areas selected should be only those in which co-operation will mutually benefit all the countries irrespective of existing economic disparities.

Domestic, Regional and Extra-regional Factors

President Rehman's effort to build co-operation in South Asia needs to be viewed within the circumstances of the major changes in the political strategic and economic ambience of both global and South Asian sub-system and a multitude of other factors.[5] Significantly the proposal was placed by the President of Bangladesh the late comer in the South Asian Comity of Nations. Keeping up this in view it would not be out of place to have a look at the major considerations that could have prompted him to come forward with the idea. The economic determinants such as deterioration in international economic situation, inflation, shrinking foreign aid flows, the spiralling price of western technology and so on were the most compelling than the political one. The universal recognition of the need for co-operation among developing countries as expressed by the group of 77, Report of the Brandt Commission could also have influenced Bangladesh President to float the idea.[6] There exists vast degree of differences among the countries of South with respect to level of development and endowment of resources. But there one must notice dynamic complementaries among these countries in resources, skills, technologies and marked opportunities. This could open new vistas of co-operation among themselves if they were prepared to implement well thought out programmes of co-operation. Co-operation among themselves would help them reduce their dependence to a few centres of the developed North. The idea of South-South co-operation got currency as a result of the action programmes adopted at the successive NAM meetings. Other factors which helped to acquire definite form and content include the activities of the group of 77 in the UN, the UN declaration and the programme of action on the NIEO adopted in 1974, the UN conference on technical co-operation in 1978, the Buenos Aires Plan of action on technical co-operation among developing countries, the Arusha Programme of Collective Self-reliance adopted by the Group of 77 in February 1979[7] and the Carcas Programme of co-operation worked out by the G-77 countries in May 1981. A good example of how the developing countries have learned to act together for mutual benefit is the establishment of a global system of Trade Preferences (GSTP) among developing countries promoted by the G-77 countries. This was in response to a crisis created by the fact that while the developed countries were dumping their manufactured goods in the markets of the developing countries, they were raising protection.

Other important factors can be summarised as follows:

(1) The demonstration effect of regional co-operation in other parts of the world; (2) The belief that it would help to enhance the capacity for collective bargaining with the rest of the world *i.e.*, the international economic environment; (3) The twin objectives of the small states in South Asia, (a) to take some of the rough edges of bilateral relations with India and (b) to increase the collective bargaining *vis-a-vis* India''.

India's Response

During the time Bangladesh presented its proposal of regionalism in South Asia, India was isolated from her neighbours due to her stand on Afghanistan, Kampuchia and Indian Ocean. In addition to the mention of the economic aspects of regional co-operation, Zia-ur-Rehman had also referred to 'peace, stability and security' in the region. The politico-strategic implications of the above-said concern need to be taken seriously. It was suspected in New Delhi that Zia mooted the idea with the direction and support of the United States and China. In his state of the union address in January 1980 President Carter disclosed the US objective of building up a ''co-operative security framework'' in South and South West Asian region. This Carter disclosure and the further elaboration of the approach by Cyrus Vance and Zbigniew Brenenski and the diplomatic activity undertaken by the United States in Islamabad and New Delhi were to meet the situation arising out of the Soviet intervention in Afghanistan.[9] Thus, the United States arrived at the conclusion that India ''has moved from a pro-Soviet invasion and called for prompt Soviet withdrawal''. However Bangladesh Foreign Secretary S.A.M.S. Kibria has strongly denied any link between its proposal and President Carter's call for creating a group of South Asian countries. In an interview he said: ''I cannot understand how such ideas crop up. The initiative has been taken by an independent country, not because of someone's inspiration. Besides it is also clear that there is no intention to form a regional military bloc behind the summoning to this conference.''[11]

Here mention should also be made to the statement made by President Zia-ur-Rehman during his four-day visit to China in 1980. He reiterated the 'principled' stand of Bangladesh in opposing the precence of foreign troops in Kampuchia and Afghanistan. He said: "we firmly believe that all foreign troops should be withdrawn immediately and unconditionally from Kampuchia and Afghanistan enabling the peoples of these two countries to decide their own future free from outside interference."[12]

Further, reiterating Bangladesh's commitment to the policy for creation of an environment of enduring peace and stability in South Asian Region, he said: "With a view to further improving the understanding and fostering more concrete co-operation among countries of the region, I have proposed a South Asian Summit meeting."[13]

The official Chinese Press, including newspapers, radio and television gave wide coverage to President Zia-ur-Rehman's visit to China.[14] Under the circumstances mentioned above India maintained that the proposal should be examined in depth in all its aspects before rushing into it.

Pakistan's Response

Pakistan also seemed to be apprehensive of the Bangladesh initiative because they thought that any framework for regional co-operation in South Asia would ultimately result in the economic and political domination of India in the region. Mistrust and suspicion grown out of the four decade old conflictual bilateral relations overshadowed Pakistani approach to the idea of South Asian Regionalism. Pakistan feared that deep involvement in a South Asian framework would gradually weaken its association with the West Asian countries. Thus it was clear that Pakistan's hesitation stemmed from 'Indo-Phobia', a fear that such an association would provide India an opportunity to institutionalise its domination over the South Asian region in general and Pakistan in particular. Pakistan's newspaper *Dawn* wrote in its editorial that "if Bangladesh's idea is forgetting anything other than an informal forum for consultation and if moves are to be made to institutionalise the arrangement, it is certain to run into snags. In view of differences of foreign policy orientations of some of the countries of South Asia and the unresolved dispute (Kashmir and Faraka) which have impeded closer co-operation between them it is very premature to think of a regional organisation."[15] However Pakistan hesitantly accepted the proposal due to the fear that, "if it did not, it could be left out of the arrangement and became isolated in the region."[16]

India and Pakistan endorsed the proposal with divergent obejctives, based on foreign policy calculations. India approved the idea because it did not want to be isolated further in the region. Moreover India found in the proposal some opportunity to draw Pakistan away from further consolidation of Pak-US-China axis. In the context of Soviet intervention in Afghanistan this was very important from the Indian standpoint. The Pakistani endorsement of the proposal was based on the Pakistani thinking that a co-operative framework in South Asia would help to "reduce the intensity of Indo-Soviet collusion aimed at the integrity of Pakistan."[17] The proposal was well endorsed by Nepal, Sri Lanka, Maldives and Bhutan.

The President of Bangladesh received positive response from those concerned in the region. This was the result of his determined effort of not less than two years. Thus, Bangladesh was entrusted with the duty of preparing the draft of a working paper. Bangladesh duly undertook the duty and prepared the working paper entitled "A Paper on the Proposal for Regional Co-operation in South Asia."

The Bangladesh Working Paper

Introductory part of the paper mentioned that, the idea of regional co-operation in South Asia is not new. Countries of the region have co-operated with one another both bilaterally and regionally under the umbrella of such forums as Economic and Social Commission for Asia and Far East (ESCAP), the Non-aligned movement and the Commonwealth.

The draft however has explained that these efforts have not fully exploited the vast potential of regional co-operation that exists and the consequential benefits that this will bring, collectively and individually, to the countries of the region. The feasibility of such co-operation was informally discussed in various capitals at different times but until recently no concrete step was taken.

After mentioning the different stages through which the proposal had passed, the working paper made the following observation:

> Preliminary exchanges have brought out clearly that regional co-operation should, on the one hand reflect the spirit of mutual trust, understanding and sympathetic appreciation of the countries of the region and, on the other, that such co-operation should be

> based on respect for the principles of Sovereign equality, territorial integrity, non-interference in the internal affairs of other nations and mutual benefit.

Then the Bangladesh draft spelt out the rationale of regional co-operation in South Asia and said that while other regions have evolved institutional arrangements for consultations on matters of mutual interest and co-operation in economic, social and cultural fields on a regional basis and had consequently benefited immensely from such co-operation, the only region which did not have any such arrangements for regional co-operation was the South Asian region which comprised one-fifth of the world population.

Commenting on the view that the South Asian countries were poor and lacked capital resources, the paper said that in other parts of the world where the countries have been economically less developed, attempts at regional co-operation have also been extensively made with varying degrees of success. The orientation and thrust of these different initiatives have not been identical. Some have attempted at customs union, others have sought technical and cultural co-operation and yet others have endeavoured to attract investments from sources outside the region.

Speaking on the structure of Economic co-operation among Developing Countries (ECDC) and Technical co-operation among Developing Countries (TCDC), that had emerged at the theatres of the Group of 77 in the UNCTAD and the NAM, the Bangladesh paper upheld regional co-operation in South Asia in these words: "Economic and Technical co-operation on a regional basis is now accepted by all developing countries as a desirable and necessary strategy within the framework of ECDC and TCDC." At the same time the paper struck a cautious note. "In South Asia, as in other regions of the world, we have countries of different levels of development, some are relatively less developed than others. Any proposal for economic co-operation must consequently be formulated with the greatest care in order to ensure that the weak are not exploited and the strong do not dominate."

The draft understood that regional co-operation would give force to the voice of the countries of the region in world Forums. The paper said: "A final argument in favour of such co-operation is that the South Asia can hope to have an effective voice in international forums. The UN system has today 150 states. It is only groups of countries -- be they big or small -- that can aspire to make a decisive impact on the decision making process in these forums. Indeed one may go so far as to say that it is only by establishing an institutional arrangement for consultation and co-ordination that the peoples of South Asia constituting one-fifth of the world population can play a role commensurate with their intrinsic global importance.''

The Bangladesh paper stood for a 'calculated and step-by-step approach' through meeting at different levels culminating in a summit and suggested that controversial political domain should be avoided and non-controversial areas of culture, science and technology should be considered for interaction as a modest beginning. It pleaded for promoting a climate of trust and confidence to bring into effect a regional approach to developmental problems. The draft favoured an early summit of the heads of the seven countries. It should also be noted that draft touched upon the political and security aspects also.[18] The Bangladesh working paper formed the basic document, on the basis of which discussions were held at the first meeting of Foreign Secretaries held in Colombo from April 20 to 23 in 1981.

Since then South Asia had several meetings at the level of Foreign Secretaries to complete the groundwork for the first meeting of the Foreign Ministers. It was held in New Delhi on 1 August 1983, signed the SAARC Declaration and affirmed ''collective resolve of the Governments to pursue actively South Asian Cooperation and to launch an Integrated Programme of Action (IPA).''[19] The first summit of the seven nation South Asian Association for Regional Co-operation was held in Dhaka on December 7 and 8, 1985. India hosted the second summit in Bangalore on November 16 and 17, 1986. The third summit was held in Kathmandu from 6 November, 1987 and the fourth took place in Islamabad on 29 and 30 December 1988.

Through the several meetings held at the bureaucratic and political level, certain areas were identified for multilateral co-operation. Similarly the institutional mechanism and funding modalities were also evolved. In the following pages an attempt has been made to review briefly the South Asian experience of regionalism within the broad framework of regional integration theory.

Notes

1. Shamsul Huq, ''Problems and Promises'' in Pran Chopra, ed., *Future of South Asia* (New Delhi, 1986), p. 67.

2. *POT*, Bangladesh Series (New Delhi), Vol. 5, August 4, 1980.
3. P.K. Mishra, "Towards a Framework of South Asian Regional Co-operation: Colombo to Kathmandu", *Foreign Affairs Report*, Vol. 31, 12 December 1982, p. 213.
4. As quoted in Kirit Bhanmik, "Dacca's Initiative", *World Focus*, Vol. 3, No. 3, March 1982, p. 10.
5. Rajaram Panda, "Recent Developments in South Asia" *Asia Pacific Community*, Vol. 24, Spring 1984, p. 65.
6. Sridhar K. Khatri, "South Asian Regional Co-operation", *Asian Survey*, Vol. XXV, No. 4, April 1985, p. 427.
7. N.N. Sachitanand, "Indian Initiative in Third World Co-operation", *The Hindu*, 11 September 1986.
8. Mohammad Ayoob, "The Primacy of the Political: South Asian Regional Co-operation in Comparative Perspective", *Asian Survey*, Vol. XXV, No. 4, April 1985.
9. *Department of State Bulletin,* March 1980, p. 65. See also S.D. Muni & Anuradha Muni, *Regional Co-operation in South Asia* (Delhi, 1984), p. 33.
10. *Department of State Bulletin*, August 1980, p. 36.
11. *POT* Bangladesh series, Vol. 5, 4 August 1980, p. 69.
12. *POT* Bangladesh series, Vol. 5, 24 July 1980, p. 1323.
13. *POT* Bangladesh series, Vol. 5, 25 July 1980, p. 1324.
14. China recognised Bangladesh in September 1975 following the coup which ousted President Mujibur Rehman who followed Pro-Soviet and Pro-India policies that did not fall in line with Beijing's aspirations. Since Zia-ur-Rehman came to power, relations with China in the cultural, scientific and economic fields had grown. In 1980 a long-term trade agreement was signed between the two countries.
15. *Dawn*, 29 May, 1980.
16. Imtiaz H. Bokhari, "South Asian Regional Co-operation: Process, Problems, Potentials and Prospects", *Asian Survey*, Vol. XXV, No. 4, April 1985, p. 374.
17. *Ibid.*, p. 390.
18. For a detailed study of Bangladesh working paper see P.K. Mishra, "Towards a Framework of South Asian Regional Co-operation: Colombo to Kathmandu", *Foreign Affairs Report,* Vol. 31, 12 December 1982, Also S.D. Muni & Anuradha Muni, *Regional Co-operation in South Asia* (Delhi, 1984), pp. 35-36.
19. Text of the Dhaka Declaration, published by the External Publicity Division, Ministry of External Affairs, New Delhi.

CHAPTER II

REGIONALISM: A THEORETICAL PERSPECTIVE

One of the most important developments in World politics in the post-World War II period has been the proliferation of regional organisations of varied nature and scope. The multiplicity of regional organisations bring home the existing reality of global interdependence, although the idea of one-world remains to be a distant dream. The question naturally arises: Are regional organisations preferable to world organisation for finding solutions to problems of peace, security, economic, social and political? The answer is that the tendency in the post-World War II period is towards "several worlds instead of one".[1]

When regionalism has become a discernible movement scholars attempted at theorising the phenomenon. Thus a plethora of explanations are available for a student of international regionalism. A wide range of interactions among the members of the international community are studied as a part of the subject. "Regionalism is a term that covers such diverse functional as well as geographical regional phenomena as European integration, NATO, the commonwealth, and the voting block in the UN."[2]

But our specific concern is regional integration which suggest a process of positive interaction among national actors within a region to harvest political, economic and security benefits. In the concept of regional integration, amalgamation is conceived as the ultimate end. The fact is that the term sounds different meanings, ideas and concepts. The dictionary meaning of integration is to "combine parts into a whole." In the literature on regionalism the term is used to denote regional co-operation, interdependence, community, regional organisation and common market. At the time of the formation of European Common Market in 1957, the term was used to represent four different things: Political Unification, Economic Unification, Economic and Political Co-operation and free trade.[3] Joseph Nye says that the concept of integration can be broken down into Economic Integration (formation of transnational society) and Political Integration (formation of a transactional political system). But even at this level the concept groups too many phenomena[4]. To some theories it is a terminal condition, to others it is a process leading to the establishment of some sort of integrated community. This difference in viewpoint is seen reflected in the definitions offered by eminent scholars who studied integration from various angles. According to Karl Deutsch integration is "the attainment, within a territory, of a 'sense of community' and of institutions and practices strong enough and widespread enough to assure, for a 'long time', dependable expectations of peaceful change among its population.[5] Deutsch's definition is not at all process oriented. His emphasis is not even on political nature of integration. He considers it as a matter of "community building". The main tasks of integration are four in number : (1) maintaining peace; (2) attaining greater multipurpose capabilities (3) accomplishing some specific task; and (4) gaining a new self image and role identity.[6]

Haas defined integration as "the process whereby political actors in several distinct national settings are persuaded to shift their loyalties, expectations and political activities towards a new centre whose institutions possess or demand jurisdiction over the pre-existing national states."[7]

In another work published in 1964, Hass conceived integration as "reflecting exclusively a process that links a given concrete international system with a dimly discernible future concrete system. If the present international scene is conceived of as a series of interacting and mingling national environments, their integration would describe the process of increasing the interaction and the mingling so as to obscure the boundaries between the system of international organisations and the environment provided by their nation-state members."[8] Later Hass revised his strictly process-oriented definition and stated that "the study of regional integration is concerned with explaining how and why states cease to be wholly sovereign, how and why they voluntarily mingle, merge and mix with their neighbours so as to lose the factual attributes of sovereignty while acquiring new techniques for resolving conflict between themselves. Regional co-operation, organisations, systems and sub-systems may help to describe steps along the way; but they should not be confused with the resulting condition."[9] John Galtung, defined integration as "the process whereby two or more actors form a new actor. When process is completed, the actors are said to be integrated. Conversely disintegration is the process whereby one actor splits into two or more actors. When the process is completed, the actors are said to be disintegrated."[10] Thus the definition of the term, integration is based upon the perception of the concerned theorists.

(i) Political Theory and Regional Integration

At this juncture it would be appropriate to make a brief mention of various approaches to the study of regional integration. Theories originated from the discipline of political science are mainly three in number *viz.*, (1) functionalism, (2) Neo-functionalism, and (3) the communication approach.

The functionalists regarded integration as a cause or consequence of co-operation in definite functional domain. The core concept is the spillover of functional co-operation from one area to another. It was conceived that states would cross over the limitations imposed by national borders and work together. Functionalism is basically an approach directed towards the problem of world order. David Mitrany[11] the father of functionalism wrote that the ever increasing complexity of Government systems had multiplicated the fundamentally technical non-political business of Governments. Such business not only generated a demand for well trained and highly qualified specialists at the national level but also contributed to technical questions at the international level. If such questions could be separated from the political sector and assigned to specialists it would help to achieve international integration. Growth of technical problems which could not be solved at the national level would lead to international co-operation in technical fields. According to Mitrany's Doctrine of Ramification development of monofunctional technical organisations in one technical field will help the proliferation of international collaboration in other technical fields. Mitrany's assumption was that functional activity would re-orient activity at international level and ultimately contribute to world peace. In the course of time monofunctional collaboration would absorb the political sector. In the words of Mitrany "the elements of a functional system could begin to work without a general political authority, but a political authority without active social functions would remain an empty temple. Society will develop by our living it, not by policing it. Nor would any political agreement survive long under economic competition, but economic unification would build up the foundation for political agreement even if it did not make it superfluous."[12] It is explained that "functionalism rests upon two fundamental assumptions: the first refers to the nature of human perceptions and motivations; the second upon the perceived nature of politics and sovereignty."[13] It is an unnatural way that the functionalists isolated the technocrats from the politicians. As remarked by Duffy and Feld what "functionalism lacked was a healthy dose of political realism to counteract the political idealism of the theory."[14] In other words "the efficiency of monofunctional technocracy did not always span legitimacy and redirection of sentiment; the spirit of nationalism, like the nation-state itself was not archaic as perceived."[15]

Although later students of integration have drawn heavily upon Mitrany's work, they have deviated very much from the mainstream functionalism. The next integrative approach is neofunctionalism, a varient of functionalism. Neofunctioanlist theory has an impressive literature on its credit. Neo-functionalism can be considered as the integration theory proper. In 1950 the French Foreign Minister Schuman announced a plan for the unification of the coal and steel industries of France, Germany and Italy and the Benulux countries. This has become the embryo of the Western European integration. Within the neo-functionalist framework the concept of "spillover", from the technical and economic to the political, was well developed. Neo-functionalism stressed the incremental growth of supranational institutions. Elites and interest group with a regional base whose membership dimensions are influenced by professional interest rather than nationality would develop within the framework of supranationality. In the place of evolutionary process incremental growth was stressed. Supranational handling of important tasks had become the major concern of neofunctionalism. EEC was created as the concrete model of neofunctionalist viewpoint. According to Nye "The neofunctionalists were federalists in functionalist clothing, pursuing federal ends through what appeared to be functionalist means."[16] Nye further adds, "The neofuncationalists avoided the approach of quiet technical self-determination that seemed to lead to political irrelevance. Rather they deliberately chose a sector that was politically important, yet that could be planned by technocrats and did not demand immediate commitment to federal institutions. They also retained some of the federalist attack on sovereignty."[17] The second major departure of neofunctionalism from classical functionalism was "its deliberate design of institutions that would lead to further integration."[18] Haas put forward his neofunctionalist concept through two classic works : *The Uniting of Europe* (1958) and *Beyond the Nation-State* (1964).[19] The combined work of Haas and Schimitter[20] proposed a complex set of variables to bring one closer to prediction. Later in 1975 he declared that major portion of the theory of neo-functionalism was obsolete[21].

Even after self-criticism and revision by prominent members of the neo-functionalist school like Haas[22], Schimitter[23] and Lindberg and Scheinglod[24] (they adapted structural functional analysis), Roger Hansen's critique of neofunctionalism is still valid. Hanson wrote that "three factors led to an overestimation of the expansiveness of functional integration in Europe of the six. They were, first, a failure to relate the process of regional integration closely enough to relevant international system factors; second, a tendency to deny rather than to investigate the discontinuity between high and welfare politics proclaimed by traditionalists; and third a failure to recognise that sizeable (and equitably distributed) economic gains would result from a common market *coordinated* by Sovereign states rather than managed by ceaselessly expanding *supernational* authorities.[25] It was criticised that in neo-functionalist theory beginning and ending were abandoned as a result of overemphasis on process. Key questions like why regional integration efforts were undertaken and what would be the final shape of regional arrangement were left without giving due attention. In the drive for the identification of independent variables all important dependent variables were neglected. It may not be incorrect to say that "neo-functionalism, in both its present and past formulations, is obsolete in terms of scientific theory."[26]

Karl Deutsch has influenced the theory of integration in a big way. His contention is that the analysis of the international transaction flows would help discover and measure international community. The application of this approach helped him to arrive at the conclusion that intra-regional transactions increased expeditiously than international transactions.[27] As a logical sequence this would accelerate the process of regional integration. However, transaction flows can only describe integration. It would not, however, cause integration.[28] Communication and transaction flows have been used to study integration by some other scholars.[29] For example Donald Puchala explored the limits and limitation of the transaction analysis and stated that: "when handled properly, transaction flows provide reasonably reliable descriptive barometers for several social, economic and political processes that occur during regional integration."[30] He provided a summary of the varieties of transaction indices and elaborated what they indicate. Most important of those discussed are the following: Percentages and proportions, relative acceptance index, foreign to domestic ratios and Michaely concentration index. The Michaely concentration index "measures intensity of geographic concentration of transaction behaviour and therefore becomes an index of preference, partnership, interdependence or dependence."[31] In the West European context this approach appeared useful because of the existence of high level of intra-regional transactions especially in the field of trade.

Deutsch expressed integration in terms of a 'security commuity'.

According to him the main tasks of integration are: (1) maintaining peace, (2) attaining greater multipurpose capabilities, (3) accomplishing some specific task, and (4) gaining a new self-image and role-identity. He further stated that all these tasks were operationally testable. The first task can be tested by the absence of paucity of specific preparation for war among the political units, regions and population within it. Evidence can be found in data on the deployment of troops, weapons and military installations; in diplomatic records and in budgetary data, in the elite and mass levels. The second task can be indicated by gross national product, per capita GNP etc. The third task can be indicated by the existence and growth of appropriate joint functions, joint institutions and joint resources and sacrifices devoted to these concrete ends. The fourth task, *i.e.*, role identity could be tested by the frequency of use of common symbols and by the creation and adoption of new symbols, by data on relevant elite and mass attitudes and so on and so forth.[32]

For the fulfilment of the above tasks, four background conditions should prevail within and among the participating political units. They are: (1) mutual relevance of the units to one another, (2) compatability of values and some joint rewards, (3) mutual responsiveness and some degree of generalised common identity or loyalty.[33] Duetsch has determined the process and instruments by which integration is approached. They are: (1) value production, (2) value allocation, (3) coercion, and (4) identification. Among these the first two refer to the production (or acquisition) and the allocation of goods and services, or relationships valued by the populations conerned, respectively. The third one means military or other enforcements, and the last concept stands for the deliberate promotion of process and sentiments of mutual identification, loyalties and 'we'-feelings.[34]

Deutsch's major concern was the preservation of peace among the integrated political units and thus he defined security community as "one in which there is real assurance that the members of that community will not fight each other physically, but will settle their dispute in some other way."[35] The post-World War II West European context represented this observation and seemed to be correct since preparation for mutual war appeared a remote possibility in West Europe.

It would be appropriate here to mention the four regionalist hypotheses put forward by Nye, concerning micro-regional organisations contribution to peace and welfare. They are: (1) restoration of multipolarity, (2) merging of small states, (3) beyond the National state and (4) new relations among states.[36] Among these four Hypotheses the last one is significant. Nye floated the hypothesis as follows:

> This regionalist doctrine does not rely so much on new institutional forums or on changing the relationships between men and states as on changing the relationships between states. The argument is that regional organisation, particularly those involving economic integration, are the best setting for functional co-operation that can make states less prone to exercise their sovereign power for violent conflict. Along with this co-operation a sense of community or positive feeling may develop between people of different states. The emphasis is not so much on diminishing sovereignty but on making it less dangerous by tying up states in a tight web or functional relationships. While such relationships would not necessarily prevent states from resorting to violence, they would introduce additional pacific influences and raise the cost of violence for particular leader.[37]

The most important aspect of the fourth hypothesis of Ney is that it does not want to curtail the sovereignty of the member countries. It is conceived that functional links among the participating countries would help to transform the relations to contribute to peace. The micro-regional organisations are less concerned about sovereignty while attempting to contribute to peace by ''raising the price of conflict, creating a sense of ''security community'' and laying a basis for integrative solutions to serious conflict. Nye tested this hypothesis in relation to European Economic Community, the Central American Common Market and the East African Common Market. He came to the conclusion that regional functional organisations ''can help to prevent violent conflict through integrative solutions or the creation of a sense of community.''[38] However he circumscribed his conclusion by adding, ''micro-regional economic organisations can supplement but not banish traditional political relationships between partner states. In the short run of decades, at least, the regionalist economic ''islands'' are not perfectly peaceful.''[39]

(ii) Economic Theory of Integration

The functionalist, neofunctionalist theories of integration are based upon the traditional customs union theory with its famous typology of free trade area, customs union, common market, economic union and complete economic integration. The origins of the economic theory of integration is attributed to Jacob Viner's book *The Customs Union*

Issue.[40] However the classification mentioned above is the contribution of Bela Balassa.[41] This theory was applied and developed in the context of the European Economic Community – a community of developed economies with a pluralistic democratic political set up.

The literature on economic integration was developed as an off-shoot of neo-classical welfare economics. The underlying principle of this theory is comparative advantage and the attainment of increased welfare through the freeing of trade. Eliminating barriers to trade among the participating countries of a customs union will create a larger market that could stimulate investment. It has been stated that the static and dynamic effects of the customs union would help to accelerate economic growth in the participating countries and this could contribute to welfare.[42] In theoretical analytical studies integration is conceived as (i) a tariff arrangement, especially a free trade area or a customs union and/or (ii) the complete or partial liberation of factor movements, and/or (iii) the co-operation in the field of economic policy, ranging from loose forms of co-ordination to complete unification. However in practice, most studies limit themselves to the well-known distinction introduced by Balassa[43]: (1) Free trade area, (2) Customs Union, (3) Common market, (4) Economic union, (5) Complete economic integration. These forms represent varying degrees of integration. In a free trade area tariffs and other restrictions are abolished among the participating states. However each member retains tariff barriers against non-members. A customs union adopts a uniform tariff for trade with the non-members, in addition to supression of discrimination. Common market is a customs union in which restrictions on factor movements are abolished. Labour and, capital can move freely within the participating system without any sort of restriction. Economic union includes the characteristics of a common market with a degree of harmonisation of economic monetary, fiscal and social policies. Total economic 'integration' would add complete unification of economic, fiscal and other policies including the adoption of a common monetary system. It would also include the setting up of a supranational authority whose decisions would be binding upon the participating countries. Bela Balassa defined economic integration as a ''process and a state of affairs. Regarded as a process, it encompasses various measures abolishing discrimination between economic units belonging to different national states: viewed as a state of affairs, it can be represented by the absence of various forms of discrimination between national economies.''[44] Economic integration as a process wrote Balassa, ''represents various measures leading to the suppression of discrimination between economic units of national states, and the resulting forms of economic integration can be characterised by the absence of discrimination in various areas.[45] At a later occasion he concluded that the "conflict between national sovereignty and economic self-interest can be resolved only if there is a political interest and political will to do so. Economic integration thus appears as part of a political process the final outcome of which is determined by essentially political factors."[46]

Kitamura observed that the "issue of economic integration at a regional level involves a choice among alternative long-term institutional arrangements in the relations of one country with others, both within the same region and outside the region. The pertinent question is what institutional framework of international relations is most conducive to accelerating the economic growth of each country as well as of the region as a whole."[47]

In the theory of economic integration a wide consensus exists on three issues:

1. that economic integration refers basically to division of labour;
2. that it involves mobility of goods or factor or both; and
3. that it is related to discrimination or non-discrimination in the treatment of goods and factors.[48]

The classical theory of economic integration matured in the context of market economies and the main arguments of the theory were based upon the doctrine of comparative advantages, "the notion that welfare will be maximised by states specialising in the production of those items in which they are more efficient or which they can produce at the least cost."[49]

The European experience of economic integration inspired the third world countries to experiment with programmes of integration to develop their national economies. In the years following the Second World War integration schemes have been launched in Latin America and Africa. However the net outcome of these schemes have been disappointing. The integration schemes of the third world countries have their own specific features that are connected with the low level of economic development and their status in the world economy. The conceptual and practical difficulties faced by third world integration projects are so many. As observed by Andre Philip, they arise in fields as diverse as the transport and communication systems inherited from the colonial period (quite unsuitable for intra-regional trade). The competitive structures of the industries and natural resources of countries potentially interested in joining regional groups, the existence of vested interest unwilling to give up the protection they now enjoy, unrealistic exchange rates, and even the shortage of basic statistical data which often rules out any reliable assessment of the probable repercussions of the integration process.[50]

Balassa attributed the limited progress in integration in developing countries to the following factors:

1. item-by-item negotiations on tariff reduction encounter considerable difficulties because of the power of special interests;

2. differences in the level of industrial development have made agreements on trade liberalisation difficult;

3. in view of the distortions in relative prices due to protection, it has been difficult to determine the benefits to be derived from integration and there has been a tendency to consider changes in the trade balance as a sign of gains or losses;

4. the Governments of the individual countries have been reluctant to proceed with integration because they are anxious to safeguard their sovereignty.[51]

Thus a rationale different from that contained in the classical theory is required for integrating the economies of the less developed states. In this respect the work done by Raul Prebisch is worth mentioning. He was the first executive secretary of the United Nations Economic Commission for Latin America (ECLA), and also he served as Secretary General of the United Nations Conference on Trade and Development (UNCTAD). In both these capacities he played a prominent role in formulating and propagating a new rationale. Prebisch and his associates believed that industrialisation was an unavoidable precondition for economic development. Import substitution should be the strategy for the same. Production of domestic substitutes, for the previously imported manufactured goods could be increased if sufficiently large market could be created. Regional integration would facilitate the creation of the required larger market. Prebisch further maintained that the required protection against competition from the industrialised world for the newly created industries could be provided by the mechanisms of regional integration. Prebisch and others also favoured the third world countries adopting strategies which would promote export-oriented industrialisation. Import substitution was considered as the first step in the direction of export promotion. The doctrine that Prebisch advanced stresses erecting barriers against trade with non-participating countries. This doctrine further maintains that LDCs should use regional economic co-operation as a means of increasing their bargaining power *vis-a-vis* already industrialised countries.[52] In other words the crux of the Prebisch's thesis can be summarised as follows: "The sustained growth of an underdeveloped economy depends on the degree to which an active process of substitution of imports by domestic production can be promoted, so as to extend the country's capacity to import to cover the acquisition of an optimum volume of capital goods and technology."[53] The declared goal of the post-Second World War European Integration was the maintenance of peace and security. This goal was pursued through the establishment of functional linkages to raise the cost of conflict. The procedure was the initiation of integration in the non-controversial areas and phased increasing of functional network to encompass higher areas. On the other hand, regional integration is sought in a third world region, for the overall development of that system. Regional co-operation is sought for the betterment of the social and economic conditions of the people and to change the unequal nature of the relationship with the developed North. In third world regions regional co-operation is considered as the mechanism through which developmental goals can be advanced further. In this context development would mean industrialisation aimed at fundamental structural change. Regional integration can help promote industrialisation. The Latin American Integration Scheme has been built around the thesis put forward by Raul Prebisch. Development strategy based on industrialisation attracted the Latin American and Carribian thinking in the 1980s. Import substitution through inviting foreign investment demanded the development approach in Latin America. Technological and other backwardness made it imperative to invite investment from the developed world. Scarcity of capital and skilled manpower necessitated external investment. External investment was attracted in the sectors of light manufacturing for import substitution and export promotion. The required foreign investment was attracted through policy instrument such as tax holidays, duty free imports of new materials etc. Thus regional co-operation is an approach for development through industrialisation by invitation and creation of a larger market. This approach is primarily concerned with the trade aspect of regional integration. Kitamura observed that, "a broadened regional market may open up quite a new dimension in the prospects of industrialisation both to individual underdeveloped countries and to the underdeveloped region as a whole.''[54] However in an integration system there exists the possibility of uneven distribution of welfare gains accrued from the integration scheme. In addition to this another important aspect of third world regional integration is the role played by the external factors.

The development linked integration scheme has been challenged by the dependency school.[55] The theory of dependence originated in Latin America and it is focused on the dependency of the third world countries on the developed centres. This theory considered the pattern of third world dependency as the most important factor in their underdevelopment. In other words third world underdevelopment is an integral component of the process of development of the developed world.[56] In the post-World War II period colonialism is perpetuated through the policies of international trade, aid finances and investment. Transnational Corporations added a new dimension to the new pattern of dependency. Industrialisation by invitation did give a good harvest to the Transnational Corporations. The investment incentives offered by the third world countries have been well utilised by the Transnational Corporations and their mentors. Even though the industrialisation by invitation recorded growth in real GDP along with per capita national income, development in the sense of structural transformation has not materialised. The ultimate effect of industrialisation by invitation was increased dependence on the developed world. It is now crystal clear that integration aimed at economic development should give top priority to reduction of dependence. The conditions of regional disparities and problems connected with trade liberalisation are also to be considered seriously. According to Constantine Vaitsos indiscriminate liberalisation would create problems in the way of effective and positive integration.[57]

This is not to say that trade liberalisation is not at all required. On the contrary, it can play a prominent role when placed in its proper context. Kitamura observes that ''regional economic integration implies broadening of the regional market and a reduction in the country's or the region's dependence on trade with the outside world at least in relative terms that is, as compared with the situation likely to prevail in the absence of integration where the tendency in the import-substitution policy has been toward discrimination against imports from within the region, this tendency will be reversed so as to increase the volume of imports from, and of exports to, the regional markets. As a consequence, not only the pattern and volume of trade, but the total volume and pattern of investment will change.''[58]

Aron Segal has aptly listed following conditions for the success of integration among the third world countries:

1. They must (the integation schemes) offer economic benefits to each unit, including an agreement on the distribution of benefits.

2. They must not threaten existing beneficial relationships or they must replace them with new ones.

3. They must not constrain the policy of nation-building.

4. They must not threaten the bases of support of existing national political elites.[59]

From the foregoing it is very clear that an integration scheme aimed at developmental goals has explicit political overtones. Economic theory of integration ignored the fundamental nexus between economics and politics. In most cases it is very difficult to maintain the distinction. Political considerations are the major determining factors in the conception and extention of integrative schemes and thus mere economic consideration is inadequate. To harvest economic benefits political aspirations of the countries involved in integration are to be given serious consideration. "Can new countries, still jealous of the newly acquired prerogatives of national independence, engage willingly in a process which will oblige them to relinquish those prerogatives in the name of a regional solidarity whose future effects they cannot discern with any certainty, but whose constraints they must certainly feel in their day-to-day experience? A decision of this kind is all the more difficult to take and to carry out whilst many of them are still suffering from internal linguistic, ethnic or religious schisms and are frequently not yet resigned to the exact delimitations of the frontiers, often artificial, which they have inherited from the colonial period."[60] The elements of the political implications of the third world integration are the following: First of all integration for development will require more complex institutions and a broader range of policies to implement the more comprehensive type of integration scheme. Secondly, the policies comprising an integration scheme deal with questions that are at the centre of political controversy in the member countries leaves little or no room for "technical" or "non-political" co-operation on virtually every issue of integration the stakes are very high. Finally, under the conditions of scarcity and immanent nationalism which prevail in most underdeveloped regions, each of the actors in the integration process will tend to take a very particularistic approach to regional negotiations.[61]

After taking into account the essential political implications of Third World Regional Integration and heavily drawing lessons from the traditional theories of integration – both political and economic – Lynn Mytelka provided three ideal types of integration schemes. According to Andrew Axline these are comprehensive models of integration formulated to suit the needs of development. He summarised Mytelka's three ideal types of integration as follows:

> The first model (type I) is a *laissez-faire* integration scheme based upon neo-classical theory and constructed on the European pattern of free trade areas and customs unions whose purpose is to expand intra-regional trade. Among underdeveloped countries, this model of trade liberalization leads to a symmetrical patterns of exchange to polarisation and to increased dependence. These resulting disequilibria create forces of instability and disintegration.
>
> The second model (type II) grows out of the need to rectify distributional problems which appear in the operation of the first model. In addition to seeking gains from trade expansion, this model includes attempts to distribute the gains of integration more equitably. Structurally, it is much more complex since it includes redistributive measures of a compensatory and corrective nature through which the problems of unequal gains and polarization can be solved collectively. Policies and mechanisms of a compensatory and corrective nature not only require a significantly higher level of commitment to act in areas of 'high politics', but also represent a very *dirigiste* approach to integration, including such measures as solidarity funds, fiscal compensation, regional development banks, and allocation of industry among countries of the region.
>
> The third model of integration (type III) goes further than the first two while including aspects of them. It responds to the problems of unequal distribution of gains and polarization through the inclusion of compensatory corrective mechanisms, but also includes measures to attack one of the principal obstacles to the success of integration and development, the condition of dependence. Thus the distinguishing characteristic of type III integration schemes is the inclusion of measures designed to overcome or reduce the pattern of dependence on metropolitan countries which constitues

> a major limiting force on the operation of the other integrative measures. A regional policy regulating foreign investment is the most obvious example of this kind of measure while regional development planning and sectoral programming go even further in overcoming dependence, as well as providing more fundamental means of regional redistribution of benefits.[62]

In spite of the fact that Mytelka's Type III model has close structural resemblence with the European pattern and neo-classical theory of integration, it is reshaped to meet the third world situations. This integration model considers the conditions of dependence and lists measures to reduce dependence to a few centres of the developed 'North'. But it is very difficult to attain the type III model. Axline has made an examination of the major political obstacles and arrives at the following conclusion:

> The nature of the process of integration among underdeveloped areas effectively undermines the expansive logic of spillover that is central to neo-functionalist theory. Rather than a logic in which economic integration moves from rather modest beginnings of technical co-operation to incrementally higher levels of political integration, the logic of integration among underdeveloped countries forsees little likelihood of success if integration is undertaken at a relatively low levels, and a greater possibility of success only if a relatively high level of political integration is undertaken at the outset. Efforts based on less comprehensive political integration are more likely to subject to a disintegrative dynamic because of built-in contradictions which lead to instability.[63]

In other words, a relatively high level of political integration is a primary requirement for an integrative scheme aimed at collective self-reliance. Nationalist, pulls and pressures, nature of the leadership, domestic political conditions, intra-regional political and economic relations and extra-regional factors play a key role in the South Asian regional system. Thus this study will look into the bilateral and external relations of the SAARC countries to assess the possibilities of a relatively high degree of political integration of an expansive, redistributive, anti-dependency integrative strategy. In this, the external aspect is considered as the first step towards regional integrative scheme elaborated above. Projection of a common regional front in dealing with external powers will have a spillover effect on bilateral relations. In other words, collective external relations will help to improve bilateral relations in South Asia. Thus external integrative aspects is of primary importance in South Asia.

The chapters that follow would study the politics of regionalism in South Asia based on the theoretical frame of reference presented above.

Notes

1. W. Friedman, *An Introduction to World Politics* (London 1956), p. 52.
2. Joseph Nye Jr. ''International Regionalism'', *World Politics*, Vol. 21, No. 1, October 1968, p. 88.
3. For a discussion of this theme see, Leon Lindberg, *The Political Dynamics of European Economic Integration* (Stanford, 1963), p. 10.
4. Nye, *op. cit.*, p. 27.
5. Karl Deutsch *et al, Political Community and the North Atlantic Area* (Princeton, 1957), p. 5.
6. Karl Deuts'ch, *Tha Analysis of International Relations (Englewood Cliffs,* 1968), p. 192.
7. Ernst B. Haas, *The Uniting of Europe: Political, Economic and Social Forces* 1950-57 (Bombay, 1958), p. 16.
8. Ernst B. Haas, *Beyond the Nation State* (Stanford, 1964), p. 29.
9. Ernest B. Haas, ''The Study of Regional Integration : Reflections on the Joy and Anguish of Pre-theorising'', *International Organisation*, Vol. XXIV, No. 4 (Autum, 1970), p. 610.
10. John Galtung, ''A Structural Theory of Integration'', *Journal of Peace Research*, Vol. 5, No. 4, 1968.
11. David Mitrany, *A Working Peace System* (Chicago, 1966) see also 'The functional approach in theoretical perspective'', *International Affairs*, July 1971, Claude, *Swords into Ploushares*; P.G. Bock, ''Functionalism and Functional Integration'', *International encyclopaedia of social sciences*; A.J.R. Groom and Paul Taylor eds., *Functionalism: Theory and Practice in International Relations* (London, 1975).
12. David Mitrany, *A Working Peace System* (Chicago, 1966), p. 97.
13. Charles A. Duffy and Werner J. Feld, ''Whither Regional Integration Theory?'' in Feld and Boyd eds., *Comparative Regional System* (New York, 1980), p. 501.
14. *Ibid.*, p. 501.
15. *Ibid.*, p. 502.
16. Nye, *op. cit.*, p. 51.
17. *Ibid.*, p. 51.
18. *Ibid.*
19. Ernst B. Hass, *Beyond the Nation State* (Stanford, 1964).
20. Hass & Schimitter, ''Economic and Differential Patterns of Political Organisation: Projections About Unity in Latin America'', *International Organisation*, Vol. 18, Autumn, 1964.
21. Haas, *The Obsolescence of Regional Integration Theory* (Berkeley, 1975), p. 1.

22. Hass, "The Study of Regional Integration: Reflections on the Joy and Anguish of Pretheorising", *International Organisation,* Vol. 24, No. 4 (Autum, 1970), pp. 607-46.
23. Philippe C. Schimitter, "A Revised Theory of Regional Integration", *International Organisation*, Vol. 24, No. 4 (Autum) 1970), pp. 840-42.
24. Lindberg and Scheingold, *Europe's would be polity: Patterns of Change in European Community* (Englewood Cliffs, 1970).
25. Roger D. Hansen, "Regional Integration: Reflections on a Decade of Theoretical Efforts", *World Politics*, Vol. 21 (January 1969), p. 256.
26. Charles A. Duffy and Werner J. Feld, *op. cit.*, p. 505.
27. J. Frankal, *Contemporary International Theory and the Behaviour of States* (New York, 1973), p. 54.
28. *Ibid.*, p. 54.
29. Donald Puchala, "International Transactions and Regional Integration", *International Organisation*, Vol. XXIV, No. 4, Autum, 1970, p. 736.
30. *Ibid.*
31. Karl W. Deutsch, *The Analysis of International Relations* (Prentice-Hall, 1968), p. 192, Details are discussed in K.W. Deutsch, *et al., Political Community and the North Atlantic Area* (Princeton, 1968).
32. *Ibid.*, p. 192.
33. *Ibid.*
34. *Ibid.*, p. 193.
35. Karl Deutsch *et al., op. cit.*, p. 2.
36. Nye, *op. cit.*, pp. 11-16.
37. *Ibid.*, p. 125.
38. *Ibid.*
39. *Ibid.*, p. 126.
40. Jacob Viner, *The Customs Union Issue* (New York, 1953).
41. Bela Balassa, *The Theory of Economic Integration* (Homewood, 1961).
42. *Ibid.*, p. 2.
43. W.G.C.M. Haack, "The Selectivity of Economic Integration Theories: A comparison of some traditional and Marxist Approaches", *Journal of Common Market Studies*, Vol. XX, No. 4, 4 June, 1983, p. 366.
44. Bela Balassa, "Toward a Theory of Economic Integration", in M.S. Wionczek, ed., *Latin American Economic Integration: Experiences and Prospects* (New York, 1966), p. 24.
45. *Ibid.*, p. 25.
46. Bela Balassa, "Types of Economic Integration", in Muchlup, ed., *Economic Integration World Wide, Regional Sectoral* (London, 1976), p. 30.
47. Kitamura, "Economic Theory and the Economic Integration of Underdeveloped Regions", in A. Wionczek ed., *op. cit.*, p. 47.
48. Fritz Machlup, "A History of Thought on Economic Integration" in Machlup ed., *op. cit.*, p. 63.
49. Harold K. Jacobson & Dusan Sidjanski, "Regional Patterns of Economic Co-operation" in Feld & Boyd eds., *op. cit.*, p. 57.

50. Andre Philip's preface in F. Kahnert *et al., Economic Integration Among Developing Countries* (Paris, 1969), p. 9.
51. Balassa in Muchlup ed., *op. cit.*, p. 27.
52. *Ibid.*, p. 61.
53. M.S. Wionczek, ''Introduction: Requisites for Viable Integration'' in M.S. Wionczek ed., *Latin American Economic Integration: Experience and Prospects* (New York, 1966), p. 1.
54. Hiroshi Kitamura, ''Economic Theory and the Economic Integration of Underdeveloped Regions'', in Wionczek ed., *op. cit.*, p. 57.
55. J. Cockfroft *et al., Dependence and Underdevelopment* (Garden City, 1972); R. Rhodes ed., *Imperialism and Underdevelopment: A Reader* (New York, 1970); C. Wilber ed., *The Political Economy of Underdevelopment* (New York, 1973).
56. Andrew Axline, *Carribbean Integration: The Politics of Regionalism* (New York, 1980), p. 15.
57. Costanine Vaitsos, ''Crisis in Regional Economic Co-operation (Integration) Among Developing Countries'', *World Development*, 1978, pp. 71-78.
58. H. Kitamura, ''Economic Theory and the Economic Integration of Underdeveloped Regions'', in M. Wionczek ed., *op. cit.*, p. 50.
59. Aaron Segal, ''The Integration of Developing Countries: Some Thoughts on Africa and Latin America'', *Journal of Common Market Studies*, June 1967, p. 263.
60. F. Kahnert, *et al.*, *Economic Integration Among Developing Countries* (OECD, 1969), p. 10.
61. Andrew Axlin, *op. cit.*, p. 32.
62. W. Andrew Axline ''Underdevelopment, Dependence and the Integration: The Politics of Regionalism in the Third World'', *International Organisation*, Winter 1977, pp. 87-88; See also Andrew Axline, *op.cit.*, 35-36.
63. *Ibid.*, p. 57.

CHAPTER III

POLITICAL ECONOMY OF SOUTH ASIA

The area that involved in this study is the South Asia which includes Bangladesh, Bhutan, India, Nepal, Pakistan, Maldives and Sri Lanka. Five of the Seven nations that constitute the region are part of the same sub-continent. Maldives and Sri Lanka are islands closely situated to the shores of the mainland.

Structural characteristics of South Asia are incomparable in the sense that no other region of the world can ever claim that much distinctiveness in geographical, physical and historical terms. The South Asian region which is more or less equal to sub-continent comprises the main portion of Asia and is larger than Europe, having a total area of two million s.q. miles placed between South-west and South-east Asia, stretching from Afghanistan in the west to Burma in the east and from Karakoram to the blue waters of the Indian Ocean. But the concept of South Asia as a distinct regional system is of very recent in origin. Even the concept of South-east Asia evolved only during the Second World War period. Later the Western writers coined the term Southern Asia, to include both what is now termed as South Asia and South-east Asia. In Michael Brecher's concept of five subordinate systems South Asia was defined as consisting of fourteen states extending from Pakistan to Indonesia.[1] But South-east Asia deserves to be viewed as a separate regional system including both China and Japan. Cantori and Speigal in their concept of 'subordinate systems of the world and their sub-divisions' identified South Asia as a distinct subordinate system consisting of India (The Core), Ceylon, Nepal, Bhutan, Sikkim, Afghanistan, Maldives Islands, Pakistan (inclusive of Bangladesh) (The periphery).[2]

In most of the difinitions Afghanistan[3] is not included in South Asia. Similarly Burma is considered as part of South-east Asia.[4] Some would like to regard Pakistan as a West Asian state. As S.P. Varma put it "the area possesses geographical continguity, if we include Afghanistan and Burma, and geographical compactness if we leave them out."[5]

In this chapter the attempt is to provide the basic socio-economic political characteristics of the South Asian countries.[6]

I. Bangladesh

Bangladesh is the most easterly of the SAARC countries, surrounded on three sides by Indian territory and Burma. On the South-east lies Burma, the one and only non-Indian border of Bangladesh. Its geographic area is 143,998 sq. kms. At the end of 1985, total population was estimated at 98,464,000. Bangladesh came to existence in 1971, before that it was the eastern wing of Pakistan, since 1947. Bengali is the national language. Islam is the state religion. Followers of Hinduism constitute a considerable minority. The total military manpower is estimated at 77000. Defence expenditure amounts to $ 158 million. Bangladesh got membership in UN in 1974 and it holds membership in 15 specialised agencies of the UN. The most important economic activity is agriculture. It provides approximately 50% of the GDP. The major food crop is rice. Wheat, sugarcane, sweet potatoes, pulses, oilseeds, bananas, tea and jute are other main agricultural products. Bangladesh is the biggest jute producing country of the world consisting of 80% of the total production of the world.

Industrial sector is very weak, contributing around 12 per cent of the GDP. Textiles, sugar factories, hosieries, aluminium works and jute based industries form the better part of the industrial sector.

Important items of exports are jute, hides, skins, leather, tea, fish and fish preparations, newsprint, paper etc. The main destinations are USA, Pakistan, UK, USSR, Mozambique, Iraq, China, Belgium, Japan and Australia. The main items of imports are machinery and transport equipment, basic manufactures, chemicals, pharamaceuticals, raw materials, food and live animals, minerals, fuels, animals and vegetable oils etc. The Main sources of imports are Japan, USA, UAE, UK, Canada, Singapore, FRG, Netherlands, India, Australia, France and USSR.

II. Bhutan

Bhutan is a landlocked country located in high mountains of the Himalayas, with India on the South and China on the North, having a territory of 47,000 sq. kms. Bhutanese speak Dzongkha and Nepali. Buddhism and Hinduism are the leading religious faiths. The political system is absolute monarchy, established in 1879.

Agriculture is the major occupation. The principal crops are rice, corn, wheat, maize, barley, millet, potatoes, pulses, tobacco, spices, fruits and forest products like wax, lac and musk. Bhutan has no industry worth the name. The major items of exports are timber, fruits, cardamom, gum, resin and handicraft. India, Middle East, Singapore and Western Europe are main destinations of exports. Raw materials, fuel, food consumer goods are imported from India. The Bhutanese economy is amalgamated with the Indian economy. Politically and economically Bhutan has a special tie-up with India. It is the integral part of the Indian defence set up. Bhutan is a member of the United Nations since 1971 and enjoys membership in eight specialised agencies. Bhutan has diplomatic relations only with India, Bangladesh, Nepal, Maldives, Kuwait, Japan and a half a dozen European countries. But it maintains embassies only in New Delhi and Dhaka besides a permanent representative at the UN and consulates in a couple of other countries.

III. India

The Union of India occupies a key position in Asia. It is bounded on the north, north-east and north-west by the mightly Himalayas, on the South-east by the Bay of Bengal and on the South-west by the Arabian sea. The southern tip is washed by the blue waters of Indian Ocean. It has a land area of 3,280.483 sq. kms. India shares its political borders with Pakistan on the west and Bangladesh and Burma on the east. The northern boundary is made up of the Sinkiang province of China, Tibet, Nepal and Bhutan. Hindi is the national language. English is also the official language of India. India is a multi-lingual state having 15 officially recognised languages. Majority of the people are Hindus. Muslims, Christians, Sikhs and Buddhists, constitute considerable minorities. India is a parliamentary democracy. Population according to 1981 census is 685,184,692. The annual rate of growth of population is estimated at 2.3 per cent.

The economy is agriculture based. The Main crops are rice, wheat, pulses, sugarcane, rapeseed, mustard, jute, cotton, tea, tobacco, coffee and rubber. The manufacturing sector accounts for 25 per cent of GDP in early 1980s. Principal industrial activities include textiles, fertilisers, chemicals, vehicles, metal industry, cement, mining (coal, iron ore, manganese, bauxite, limestone, chromium, lead concentrates, zinc, diamonds, gypsum, crude petroleum and natural gas). Exports consists of textiles, pearls, precious and semi-precious stones, machinery, tea, leather and leather goods, iron ore, fish, crustaceans, iron and steel, jute manufactures, metal manufactures, chemicals, spices, cashew nut, cereals, tobacco, coffee, sugar, silver, wheat, fruit, vegetables and handicrafts. Main destinations include USA, Japan, UK, USSR, FRG, Netherlands, Belgium, France, Hong Kong, Italy, Kuwait, Saudi Arabia, UAE, Iran, Australia, Switzerland, Poland, Egypt, Malasia, Sudan, Yugoslavia, GDR, Czechoslovakia.

Imports, on the other hand, cover mineral fuels, machinery, transport equipment, textile fibres, edible vegetable oil, pearls, precious and semi-precious stones, non-ferrous metals, organic chemicals, resins, plastics, crude fertilisers and wheat. The main suppliers of these items are USA, Iraq, Germany, Malaysia, France, Canada, Belgium, Saudi Arabia, Netherlands, Italy, UAE, Australia, Singapore, Switzerland, Poland, GDR, Czechoslovakia, Sudan and Yugoslavia.

India took membership in the United Nations in 1945, three years before independence from the British colonial rule. India has membership in 16 specialised agencies.

IV. Maldives

Maldives is an archipelago in the Indian ocean, to the west of Sri Lanka and South-west of India. It consists of 2000 small islands 12 coral atolls and area is 298 sq. kms. The archipelago spreads out around 300 miles north to south.

Maldives got independence on July 26, 1965 and it became a republic in November 1968. Dominant religion is Islam. Divehi is the national language. Population is 1,68,000. Most of the people are engaged in fishing. Fishermen constitute 44 per cent of the labour force. It has been the main source of income. It accounts for nearly one-third of the GDP. Fish processing is the main industry. Since 1970s tourism is a major source of foreign exchange. It is recorded that over 29,000 tourists, mostly from western Europe--FRG, Italy, France, Sweden -- visit Maldives every year. Coconuts, bread, fruit, finger millet, sweet potato, cassava, taro maize and sorghum are the main agricultural products. Consumer goods, intermediate and capital goods, petroleum products are the main items of import. These are imported mainly from Japan, UK, Thailand and Sri Lanka.

Fresh fish, dry salted fish, garments, manufacturing goods are the main exports and destinations of these goods are Japan, Sri Lanka, Thailand and Singapore. Maldives is a member of the United Nations since 1968 and it enjoys membership in fourteen specialised agencies of the U.N.

V. Nepal

The kingdom of Nepal is situated between India and China in the Southern slope of the Himalayas. Land-locked Nepal's total area is 147,141 sq. kms. and population is 16,107,000. Hinduism is the state religion. People speaks Nepali.

Nepal is well-endowed in forest riches and quartz deposits. Industries' total contribution to GDP is 10 per cent. Industries are mainly small scale. Important industrial activities include textiles, paper, pulp, cement, leather goods, foot-wear, cigarettes, brewing, food-processing, jute, pharmaceuticals and agricultural tools. The Government is offering liberal incentives to attract foreign investments.

Agriculture constitutes 60 per cent of the GDP. Rice, maize, wheat, sugarcane, millet, barley, oil seeds, tobacco, jute, fruit and vegetables are the main agricultural products. Basic manufacturing, machinery and transport equipment, food and live animals, chemicals, mineral fuels, miscellaneous manufactures and raw materials are imported from India, Japan and USA. Rice, raw jute cuttings, timber, hessian, sacking, twine and ghee are exported to India, USA, Japan, Singapore, Hong Kong and FRG. Nepal got its membership in the United Nations in 1955 and it holds membership in 14 specialised agencies of the UN. Nepal is geo-politically part of India and strategically important in the defence of the Indo-Gangetic Plain.

VI. Pakistan

The Islamic Republic of Pakistan came into existence in 1947, following the partition of the subcontinent into two states, India and Pakistan. Its area is 796,095 sq. kms. and population 98,971,000. Official language is Urudu. Pakistan is having border with Afghanistan, China, Iran and India.

Agriculture is the mainstay of the Pakistan economy. It is nearly 60 per cent of the GDP. Wheat, maize, barley, millet, sorghum, sugarcane, tobacco, groundnuts, pulses, rapeseed, sesame, fruit and vegetables, cotton are the major crops. Industries are developed with indigenous resources and foreign know-how. Industries constitute 24 per cent of the GDP. Textiles, chemicals and fertilisers, food-processing, steel, oil, and natural gas, mining (coal, chromite, limestone, gypsum, silver, silica, sand, fireclay, celastile, rock salt, ochres, iron ore), electricity, energy are the main industries.

Rice, cotton (raw cotton, cotton fabrics, cotton yarn, cotton waste, cotton thread), carpets, rugs, leather, drugs, chemicals, clothing, hosiery, fish and fish preparations are the main items of export. Hong Kong, Japan, FRG., Saudi Arabia, USA, UK, Italy. UAE, Iran, France, Sri Lanka, Kuwait, Bahrein, Australia are the main destinations. Trade with India was resumed in 1975 and it involves only public section of Pakistan. Machinery and transport equipment, oil, iron and steel, chemical fertilisers, vegetable oils, sugar, paper, pharmeceuticals are the important import items. Japan, USA, Kuwait, UK, FRG, Saudi Arabia, Netherlands, France, UAE, Italy, China, Australia, Malaysia are the main import sources.

Pakistan took membership in the United Nations in 1947 and it is having membership in 16 specialised agencies of the UN.

VII. Sri Lanka

Sri Lanka having an area of 65,610 sq. kms. and a population of 1,60,76,000 is an island separated from India by the shallow Palk Strait and the Gulf of Mannar. It is bounded on the west by the Palk Strait and the Gulf of Mannar on the north and east by the Bay of Bengal and the South by the Indian ocean. It became independent from the British colonial rule in 1948, and since then a member of the commonwealth. Sinhala and Tamil are the languages. Buddhism and Hinduism are the dominant religions.

Agriculture contributes nearly one-third of the GNP. Main food crops are rice, cassava, sweet potatoes, potatoes, maize, millet and onions. Sri Lanka is the world's second larget producer and exporter of tea. Other important cash crops are dry beans, seasame, sugar cane, cashewnuts, coffee, cocoa, tobacco and spices.

Petroleum, machinery and equipment, food items, textiles, chemicals, paper are imported from Japan, UK, Saudi Arabia, Iran, India, USA, Singapore, Australia, China, Hong Kong, Canada, France, USSR and Burma. Tea, rubber, coconuts and precious stones are exported to countries like USA, UK, Japan, FRG, China, Pakistan, Saudi Arabia, South Africa, Canada, Australia, USSR, Netherlands, France, Italy, Kuwait and Taiwan. Sri Lanka joined the United Nations in 1955 and has membership in fifteen specialised agencies.

Notwithstanding its colossal land area of 4.48 mn sq. kms. and its multi-racial, multi-religious, multi-lingual population the South Asian regional system has a character of its own by any measure including history and geography. All the countries in the subcontinent were dominions, colonies or protectorates of Britain. In every state of the sub-continent, the English language continues to enjoy a prominent position in the sense that it is widely used in Government offices and educational institutions. In fact, English is the language of the elite in South Asia. This is not the only gift of the British colonial domination. Administrative structure and educational system still remain under the strong influence of the British rule. But the English language has got an exceptional role in South Asia as a medium of communication and instrument of mutual understanding. Moreover all the states of the region are members of the non-aligned club.

Despite the uniformity mentioned above there exists vast disparity in terms of area, population and economy. Of the combined land area of the sub-continent 73.26 per cent belong to India, succeeded by Pakistan (17.73), Nepal (3.28), Bangladesh (3.21), Sri Lanka (1.46), Bhutan (1.05) and the Maldives (0.01). The total population of the seven is 930 mn, which is one-fifth of that of the globe. Of that India accounts for 77.11 per cent, Bangladesh 10.20 per cent, Pakistan 9.18 per cent, Nepal 1.69 per cent, Sri Lanka 1.67 per cent, Bhutan 0.13 per cent and Maldives 0.02 per cent.[7] The growth rate of population is 2.2 during the 1970-77 period compared with the growth rate of 1.7 per cent of the world as a whole.[8] The subcontinent is rich in manpower resources. The region had a labour force of 298 million in 1975. The growth rate of the labour force is 2 per cent.[9] The economies of the region exhibit low rate of economic growth. Low level of per capita income is noticeable.

Agriculture

In the economies of the South Asian countries agriculture occupy an important place. Agricultural sector absorbs major chunk of the labour force in these countries. Besides agriculture accounts for very large portion of the GDP. The growth rate of agriculture is less than the growth rate of population in some countries of the sub- continent. Only India and Sri Lanka are self-sufficient in food-grain-production. Food grains are imported into these countries. One of the reasons for stagnation of agriculture and rural poverty is the unequal distribution of land. This results in a relatively small number of farms having large land holdings and a very much larger number having very small holdings. Land reforms which could have reduced these inequalities have not been effectively carried out.[10]

Manufacturing Sector

Industrial production has been increasing in all states of the region. As a result the export of manufactured goods have been growing in some states especially in Pakistan and India. When compared to other third world regions, involvement of multinationals in the manufacturing section is very small. However in the case of some states of the region external public debt is very big. The per capita income is very low. In fact large chunk of the population live in deplorable conditions of poverty and they have income which are considerably below the per capita income. Most of the people are struggling to meet even the basic necessities.

The rate of growth of agriculture has been adversely affected by unfavourable conditions of weather in most of the countries of the sub-continent. Savings are very low and fiscal policies of Government are expansionary and hence double digit levels of inflation. The South Asian states are facing many common problems in the field of trade, with both developed market economies and socialist countries. These countries are also facing problems with regard to transfer of technology, dealings with transnational corporations and in all questions pertaining to North-South Dialogue.

It is clear that the common problem facing these countries is poverty. Other important challanges are illiteracy and a host of social inequalities. The UNCTAD identified 36 LLDCs at the end of 1984, among these were included Bangladesh, Bhutan, Nepal, and the Maldives. The average per capita income of the countries in this region is just US $ 245.[11]

The economies of most of the South Asian countries are competitive rather than complimentary. But this was not so during the British rule. For example, during the colonial rule jute was produced by East Bengal and jute mills were situated in the West Bengal. Just like that the area now comprising Pakistan produced raw cotton while it was processed in cotton mills situated in areas which became part of independent India. This complementariness was reversed with the withdrawal of the British.

Indian economy is well placed when compared to her neighbours. This is because of the rather sound resource potential and its wise mobilisation. This led to the development of a fear complex in the minds of her neighbours that any sort of understanding with India would ultimately lead to the dominance of India in the region. This fear led the South Asian periphery to adopt irrational economic policies. They preferred to have economic collaboration with outside powers like Japan and Western Europe. The main intention behind this policy was to undermine India's economic dominance in the region. But this has adversely affected all the South Asian economies.

From the analysis made so far it is clear that India is placed at the pivot in South Asia. As it was stated the whole region is "India dominated" and "Indocentric" because of its location, size and resource potentials. India possesses a coastal line of 3,500 miles and a land frontier of 9,400 miles. From Himalayas down to the tip of Kanyakumari the range is 2,000 miles. Its population exceeds 70 crores. All these factors together make India the core of South Asia.

Socio-Political Profile

The successive invasions of external powers like the Turks, Mughals and the Europeans for over a thousand years had its mark on the ethnic configuration and cultural composition of the region.

North-Indians and Pakistanis belong to the Indo-Aryan cultural stock. Monglo-Dravidians constitute a sizable section of the people of Eastern India and Bangladesh. Mongolian races live in Nepal and the adjoining Indian territories. South India as a whole and a part of Sri Lanka are occupied by Dravidians. While the Sinhales are of Aryan origin.[12] Lingustic differences and similarities are more complex and sophisticated than that of ethnic homogeneity and diversity. Urdu is the national language of Pakistan. Punjabi, Pushto, Sindhi are also spoken by the people in different parts of Pakistan. A large chunk of North Indian people also use these languages. Urdu-speaking Pakistanis understand perfectly Hindi-speaking Indians. All these languages are that of the Indo-Aryan language group with an admixture of Turko-Iranian (Baluchi and Pusthu). Similarly, Bengali is the national language of Bangladesh. At the same time, it is the lingua franca in the Indian state of West Bengal. 25 per cent of the Sri Lankan population and the Indian state of Tamil Nadu speak Tamil. Nepali is spoken in the Darjiling District of West Bengal. "The linguistic dimension of inter-state relation in South Asia is so puzzling and novel that students of international politics including those resident in these countries, have failed to grasp the full implications and ramifications of the linguistic affinities cutting across international boundaries... The linguistic boundaries in South Asia do not coincide with international boundaries."[13]

Hinduism is the major religion in South Asia. India and Nepal are predominently Hindu. In secular India, Hindus form 83 per cent of the total population. In Bangladesh, Pakistan and Sri Lanka, they constitute a considerable minority. Islam is the state religion of Pakistan and Bangladesh. Maldives is also a Muslim country. Muslims are minorities in India and Sri Lanka. Buddhism is professed and practised in Sri Lanka. Buddhism prevails among the people of Nepal, Sikkhim, and the Eastern part of the Himalayas. As a result of the British rule, Christianity also has got followers in South Asia, especially in India and Sri Lanka. "In the world state system, there is no comparable example of proximity of states containing adherents of so many different religions. The problem is made more complicated by the fact that substantial religious minorities exist in every state. Religion thus provides a cause of division as well as unison among the South Asian peoples as adherents of one faith have a natural affinity with their co-religionists which they cannot extend towards believers in other faiths. Religion also becomes a factor in the generation of communal feelings."[14] For over a century the South Asian sub-continent was one not only physically but politically also. Western imperialism brought the entire region under the unified control of Great Britain. This resulted in the development of common political, legal and administrative institutions. The basic characteristics of the nationalist movement for freedom in all parts of the region were identical, notwithstanding the growth of separatist tendencies. The educational background, aspirations and world view of the leaders of the freedom movement were more or less the same. All of them were western educated, English-knowing middle calss elites of the sub-continent. They imbibed the indispensible qualities of 20th Century English liberalism and hatred towards imperialist subjugation. "The similar socialisation of the elites has evolved certain common external national role conceptions in the regional context. For example, the ruling elites of all the states are concerned about the maintainence of *status-quo*."[15] With the withdrawal of the British, the overall control from one centre bid fare-well to the region for ever. Four new national entities came into existnece in the sub-continent. One among them named Pakistan was carved out of the Muslim majority area of the British India's Western and Eastern flank. Later, in 1971, East Bengal, part of Pakistan but separated by thousands and thousands of miles of Indian soil went away to establish an independent sovereign state of its own. Thus South Asia witnessed the birth of Bangladesh. It may be noted that the region has undergone a reverse historical process. The Indian sub-continent which was one country upto 1947 was partitioned into two in that year. It split further into three in

1971. In retrospect, therefore, the region was largely integrated in 1947. But the region was subsequently fragmented into completely independent political entities.[16]

Leo E. Rose has pointed out another aspect of the sub-continent that the sub-continent was never a unified political entity prior to 1947 except under alien rulers with a world view distant from that of Hindu India. In this regard, India contrasts sharply with China, Japan and several South East Asian States.[17]

It is very difficult to distinguish these countries from one another if we consider other spheres of importance. As noted earlier, they have got common religions. Hinduism, Islam, Buddhism, Sikkhism and Christianity are shared by all the countries of the region. Ethnically too, there is considerable amount of overlapping. Aryan, Dravidian, and Mangoloid blood are mixed up to blur any sort of ethnic demarcation. Similarly, languages are crossing frontiers. "Geographical compactness and contiguity, added to the British rule of finding expression in political and legal systems and administrative institutions and the overlapping of religions and languages, which make the countries of South Asia so indistinguishable from each other."[18]

The economic policy adopted by various South Asian countries have also got similarities. The approach has been to build up capitalism through centralised planning with a tingue of socialism. The emphasis is on the development of a mixed economy giving equal importance to public and private sectors. But the remnants of old pattern of economic structure make its presence felt everywhere. "The economies were characterised by the simultaneous existence of dominant feudal and prefeudal sorts of modes of production along with a marginal land, in some cases, a dependent modern sector."[19] This is because of the economic policy of the colonial master. During the colonial period, South Asian ecnomics were mere appendages of the British Economy. The net result was deindustrialisation of South Asian economies.

Geography, religion, ethnically and language are discussed as the unifying factors. At the very same time, they are operating as divisive factors. Even though the British colonial administration was a unifying factor it also laid the seeds of conflict. Their divide and rule policy sowed the seed of differences between Hindus and Muslims. Hindus and Muslims had been living in India as brothers and sisters for centuries. The brotherly affection and harmonious relationship existed among these two religious groups were destroyed by the British policy of instigating communal feelings of the fanatics on both the sides. The British succeeded in implanting a sense of insecurity in the Muslim psyche that the Muslims could not live in independent India as co-citizens with the Hindus. This led to the two-nation theory and the bloody partition. As a result, "an unnatural and absurd state system was brought into being by means of partition of the sub-continent and the creation of a disjointed Pakistan. The British rulers, no doubt played the most significant role in this partition, which, as is well known, led to a series of conflicts and hampered co-operative ventures in the region."[20] Partition failed to patch up the once deteriorated relation between the Hindus and Muslims. The flow of refugees further worsened the whole situation. There remained considerable amount of Hindus in Pakistan and Muslims in India. Pakistan Muslims still continue to worry about the fate of their Muslim brothers in India. Similarly, the Hindus of India happened to be worrying about the fate of their co-religionists in Pakistan. "In the history of the world, there are numerous examples of sovereign states projecting a religious identity on the external stage and acting in concert with states with a similar religious complexion. With the decline of the role of religion in moulding the behaviour of individuals and society, the type of international behaviour, has however, been superseded by the emerging pattern of international politics based on politico-economic calculus. The leaders of South Asian states are, by and large, still universal in this calculus of economic rationality and national strategy. They put their faith in the simple rule of the thumb which tells them that only their co-religionists are their best friends."[21]

The presence of religious and linguistic minority groups across national boundaries acted as irritant factor in the past. The future is also clouded by these factors to a great extent. There exists a clear emphasis on particularistic religions, ethnic and linguistic components of social fabric rather than on universalistic goals and tendencies in the nation building processes. The emphasis is on Islam and Urdu in Pakistan, Islam and Bengali in Bangladesh, Buddhism and Sinhalese in Sri Lanka, Hinduism in Nepal and Buddhism of different sects and varieties in Bhutan. All this resulted in the emergence of dominant ethnic groups in the countries of South Asia. Consequently, the politics of nation building in each of these countries gave rise to many complex problems with repercussions extending across national boundaries particularly in Pakistan, India and Bangladesh; directly impinge upon the mutual state-to-state relations. Communal relations in South Asia necessrily possess a minority-majority dimension cutting across national boundaries[22].

Political instability is a marked characteristic of South Asia. India stands as an exception. India has not undergone too frequent political changes as is seen in other parts of the region. Moreover, India is adhered to the political philosophy of democracy and social philosophy of secularism, even though there are pitfalls in her secularistic orientation. But this is not the state of affairs in other South Asian States. In Sri Lanka Governmental power has alternated between the United National Party (UNP) and the Sri Lanka Freedom Party (SLFP). After the 1977 election there occurred a change in the political system also. Parliamentary form of Government gave way to French model of Presidential type of Government. While in Pakistan military bureaucratic establishment is well entrenched, in Nepal monarchy is well rooted but they are in search of viability in their political system. Bangladesh also witnessed massive political change in 1975. These differences in political system and constitutional instability have got its own share in maintaining intra-regional differences.

There are differences with respect to the foreign policy preferences too. Anti-Indian feelings are prevalent in the foreign policy preferences of these states. They feel that any sort of co-operation with India would block development of separate identity which they desire very much. They fear the proverbial big-brother attitude of India. Moreover, the above-said frequent changes in the political system and Government always stand in the way of nation building. Poverty and unemployment have been taking a new turn day after day. The credibility of the Government may be questioned by powerful divisive forces at any time. To check such an eventuality leaders of these countries used to instigate anti-Indian feelings purposefully.

But any standard India is the dominant power in this region. It is not an exaggeration when one scholar called this region Indo-centric and India-dominated. No doubt India has got a pre-eminent position in the region economically, militarily and technically. Ideologically too, India has got a sound footing. Moreover, India is the only state having common frontier with all these states. No other state in the region shares common border with the others.

Notes

1. Cited in Yogesh Atal, "Subordinate state systems and Nation-set: tools for the analysis

of external milieu", in S.P. Varma and K.P. Mishra eds., *Foreign Policies in South Asia* (Jaipur, 1969), pp. 41-44 and S.U. Kodikara, "Regional roles and behaviour in South Asia: A Theoretical Framework for Regional co-operation", in Babani Sen Gupta ed., *Regional Co-operation and Development in South Asia*, Vol. I (New Delhi, 1986), pp. 31-36.

2. Louis J. Cantori and Steven L. Spiegal, *The International Politics of Regions* (New Jersey, 1970), p. 9.
3. Pakistan opposes Kabul's moves to seek SAARC membership. Bangladesh also opposed the entry of Afghanistan. *Bangladesh Time*, 28 July 1987.
4. Burma has rejected an Indian suggestion to join the SAARC, *Tribune*, 17 December 1987.
5. S.P. Varma, *op. cit.*, p. 342.
6. This section is prepared on the basis of data collected from various sources such as, World Development Report 1987, Financial Express (various issues), Statistical Year Book for Asia and Pacific 1985, Handbook of International Trade and Development Statistics, 1986· Ministry of Commerce (Government of India) Annual Reports, IMF Direction of Trade (Various issues), UN Economic and Social Survey of Asia and Pacific, 1981, IMF International Financial Statistics Year Book 1984, Facts on Sri Lanka, Published by the Government of Sri Lanka.
7. Vidya Bir Singh Kansaker, "The Demographic Dimension of Regional Co-operation in South Asia", *Regional Studies*, No. 3, Spring 1985, p. 78.
8. M.L. Qureshi, "South Asian Economies During 1970s: An overall view", *South Asian Studies*, Vol. I, No. 1, January 1984, p. 9.
9. *Ibid.*, p. 10.
10. *Ibid.*, p. 12.
11. "South Asia – Regional Co-operation", *Asian Security*, 1980, p. 146.
12. S.P. Varma, "South Asia as a Region" in S.P. Varma and K.P. Misra eds. *Op. cit.*, p. 374 and Ajit Singh Sarhadi, *India's Security in Resurgent Asia* (New Delhi, 1979), p. 72.
13. P.C. Mathur, Virendra Narian and M.V. Lakhi, "Intra-regional Relations: A Study in Infra-structural Determinants" in S.P. Varma and K.P. Misra eds. *op. cit.*, p. 97.
14. *Ibid.*, p. 94.
15. Sivananda Patnaik, "Sri Lanka and the South Asian Sub-system: A Study of Macro International Politics." *India Quarterly* (New Delhi), Vol. 35, No. 2, April-June 1980, p. 138.
16. Satish Kumar, "Trends in Regional Developments in South Asia," in M.S. Rajan and Shivaji Ganguly eds., *Great Power Relations World Order and Third World* (New Delhi, 1981), pp. 271-72.
17. Leo E. Rose, "India", in Wayne Wilcox, Leo E. Rose and Gavin Boyd eds., *Asia and the International System* (Boston, Mass, 1961), p. 238.
18. S.P. Varma, *op. cit.*, p. 347.

19. S.D. Muni, "India and Regionalism in South Asia: A Political Perspective", in Bimal Prasad ed., *India's Foreign Policy in Continuity and Change* (New Delhi, 1979), p. 110.
20. *Ibid.*, p. 109.
21. P.C. Mathur *et al*, *op. cit.*, pp. 92-93.
22. S.D. Muni, *op. cit.*, p. 111.

CHAPTER IV

REGIONAL CO-OPERATION AND DEVELOPMENT: THE SOUTH ASIAN EXPERIENCE

This chapter sketches the modalities and mechanisms SAARC has evolved for the purpose of implementing, co-ordinating, and monitoring its activities and assesses the progress the association has made so far in the agreed upon areas of co-operation. Also an attempt is made to relate the course of SAARC co-operation to the theme of community formation.

While elaborating the Mytelka model of regional integration Axiline has identified three elements of third world integration which he considered as the political implications of economic integration. These implications are related to the institutions and policies comprising an integrative mechanism and the negotiations underlying the adoption of these institutions and policies. Axline has summarised these elements thus:

> First of all integration for development will require more complex institutions and a broader range of policies to implement the more comprehensive type of integration scheme. Secondly, the fact that these policies deal with questions that are at the centre of political controversy in the member countries leaves little or no room for "techinical" or "non-political" co-operation. On virtually every issue of integration the stakes are very high. Finally, under the conditions of scarcity and imminent nationalism which prevail in most underdeveloped regions, each of these actors in the integration process will tend to take a very particularistic approach to regional negotiations.[1]

In relation to these three themes, SAARC institutions and policies are discussed in this chapter. The first meeting of the Foreign Secretaries (Colombo, April 21-23, 1981), evolved the following principles to steer the emerging framework of multilateral co-operation:

(1) Principles of unanimity should be the basis for decision-making;

(2) Bilateral and contentious issues should be excluded from the delibrations; (3) Regional co-operation is not intended to or expected to be a substitute for bilateral and multilateral co-operation but could complement both; nor should it be inconsistent with bilateral and multilateral obligations; and (4) Regional co-operation should be based on respect for the principles of sovereign equality, territorial integrity, political independence, non-interference in the internal affairs of other states and mutual benefit.[2]

This meeting witnessed the coming into limelight the differences between India and Pakistan on the one side and the small states on the other. Both India and Pakistan opposed any sort of institutional framework at this stage. It should be noted here that Bangladesh, Bhutan, Maldives and Nepal were more enthusiastic on an early summit and other forms of institutionalisation. Sri Lankan approach was positive and favoured a slow moving institutional framework. While India stood for a step-by-step course, Pakistan was by and large sceptical in the sense that the Pakistani delegation was concerned with airing regional differences rather than highlighting the commonalities.

The Foreign Secretaries met in Kathmandu for the second time from November 2 to 4, 1981 in accordance with the decision of their first meeting in Colombo. In this meeting institutional aspect received little attention. In the Islamabad meeting (August 7-9, 1982) Bangladesh pressed for a meeting of the Foreign Ministers before the end of the year. Other countries seemed to agree that it should be called at some stage but were divided on when exactly it should be called. Bangladesh seemed to be evoked support for an early meeting from countries like Bhutan, Maldives and Sri Lanka.[3]

India was not in favour of a Foreign Ministers Conference during the year. India was not opposed to such a conference, but it thought that a lot more remained to be done before it could be called for achieving results. India maintained that concrete and action-oriented programme had yet to be worked out. Planning experts of the Seven nations had also not yet established contacts. Preparatory works on many areas including regional tourism remained to be done. The Indian suggestion was that a few more meetings should be held at the Foreign Secretaries level before the Foreign Ministers were requested to meet.[4]

Pakistan too appeared to be favouring a step-by-step approach to evolve the concept of South Asian Co-operation. The South Asian Nations should move with measured pace, consolidating the gains already made.

A three tier institutional arrangement took its shape in the first meeting of the Foreign Ministers of the Seven nations in New Delhi in 1983 and it was incorporated in the New Delhi Declaration signed by the Foreign Ministers in August 1983. The institutional arrangement included the following: (1) The Technical Committees; (2) Action Committees ; and (3) The Standing Committee.

Technical Committee was entrusted with the duty of the implementation, co-ordination and monitoring of the programmes in each area of co-operation. All the member countries are representing in the technical committees with the following terms of references:

(a) determination of the potential and the scope of regional co-operation in agreed areas,
(b) formulation of programmes of action and preparation of prospects,
(c) determination of financial implications of the sectoral programmes of action,
(d) formulation of recommendations regarding the appointments of costs,
(e) implementation and co-ordination of sectoral programmes of action,
(f) monitoring of progress of implementation.

The Technical Committee shall be required to submit periodic reports to the Standing Committee. The chairmanship of the Technical Committee shall be rotated among the participating countries in alphabetical order, every two years.

If and when considered necessary, the technical committee may use the following mechanisms and modalities: (a) Meeting of Heads of National Technical Agencies, (b) Meetings of experts in specific fields, and (c) Contacts amongst recognised centres of excellence in the region. These countries may be reinforced and extended as considered feasible and desirable for the optimal use of the resources of the region for meeting the requirements of the co-operation planning.

The second tier is the action committees. In the case of projects involving more than two countries but not all the member countries, action committees comprising the countries concerned may be set up for their implementation, with the prior approval of the Standing Committee.

The third tier in the institutional arrangement, envisaged in the Delhi Declaration, is the Standing Committee at the level of Foreign Secretaries for the co-ordination and the monitoring of the programme with the following terms of reference:

(a) approval of projects and programmes and the modalities of their financing, (b) determination of inter-sectoral priorities and over-all co-ordination of programme of action, (c) mobilization of regional and external resources, and (d) identification of new areas of co-operation based on appropriate studies. The Standing Committee shall meet as often as is deemed necessary but at least once a year. The Standing Committee is intended to provide necessary support services for meeting of Ministers. The Standing Committee shall make a reference, as and when necessary, to the Foreign Ministers for decisions of policy guidelines of projects/programmes as well as the authorisation of modalities for financing.

The first ever meeting of the heads of state or Government held in Dhaka adopted the Charter of the Association. The Charter spelt out the framework of South Asian regional co-operation duly enumerating the objectives, principles and mechanism. The Charter is only a modified version of the New Delhi Declaration, adopted by Foreign Ministers in July 1983. However the preamble got a little reshaping. The eight objectives and two principles are the same as listed in the Delhi Declaration. The part on institutional arrangement reformulated and updated.

Article III of the Charter related to the meetings of the Heads of State or Government. As per the article the periodicity of the summit meeting would be once a year more often as and when considered necessary by the member states. Significantly, the decision to increase the frequency of the summit as against two years as suggested by Foreign Ministers meetings to once a year was taken on the plea of General Zia-ul-Haq.

A Council of Ministers (Article IV) consisting of the Foreign Ministers of the member States was established with the following functions : (a) Formulation of the policies of the Association, (b) Review the progress of co-operation on agreed upon areas, (c) Decision on new and additional mechanisms, (d) Establishment of additional mechanism under the Association as deemed necessary, and (e) Decision on other matters of general interest on the Association. The Standing Committee, adapted from the New Delhi Declaration, found its place in Article V in a modified form, to monitor and co-ordinate programmes, approval of projects and funding modalities, determine inter-sectoral priorities, mobilise regional and external resources and identify new areas of co-operation based on appropriate studies. It should submit periodic reports to the Council of Ministers and take reference to it as an when necessary for decisions on policy matters and held its meeting as often as deemed necessary.

The technical committee and action committee got its place in the Charter as Article VI and VII respectively. Provision for the Secretariat (Article IX) was incorporated in the Charter and infra-structural details left to be settled by the Council of Ministers. Article X dealt with the general provisions. In this Article concept of unanimity was further emphasised. In like manner the Charter decided to exclude bilateral and contentious issues from its delibrations. The SAARC leaders agreed to open the SAARC Secretariat at Kathmandu, Nepal, on 16 January, 1987.

Structure and Function of SAARC Secretariat

The Foreign Ministers of the member countries signed the Memorandum of Understanding on the establishment of the Secretariat, in the presence of the Heads of State of Governments. The leaders agreed on the arrangements with regard to the establishment of the SAARC Secretariat in pursuance of Article VIII of the SAARC Charter.

The Secretariat located in Kathmandu, shall comprise a Secretary General and professional and general services staff and contain an appropriate number of funcitonal units to be called Divisions (Article IV). Article V of the Understanding deals with the modalities of the appointment of the Secretary General, who shall be appointed by the Council of Ministers upon the nomination by a member state on the basis of the principle of rotation in alphabetical order. The appointment of the Secretary General shall be for a non-renewable tenure of two years. He shall hold the rank and status of Ambassador.

In the event of the Secretary General being unable to serve his full term, the unexpired portion of his term shall be filled in by the nominee of the Government of the Country from which the Secretary General comes upon the apporoval of the Council of Ministers. Until this arrangement is made the Director from the Country next in alphabetical order shall be the Officer-in-charge.

As the Head of the SAARC Secretariat, the functions and powers of the Secretary General are eight in number, *viz.*:

1. The Secretary General shall be responsible for conducting the work of the Secretariat including the co-ordination and monitoring of SAARC activities;
2. Submit staff rules and Financial Regulations to the Standing Committee for approval of the Council of Ministers;
3. Act as the channel of communication and linkage, when so empowered by the Standing Committee, between SAARC and

other international organisations on matters of mutual interest. In doing so, the Secretary General shall be guided by the decision of the Council of Ministers that initiatives for collaboration with external agencies should stem from SAARC itself based on its own determination of priorities and keeping in mind the relevant provisions of the SAARC Charter;

4. Assist in organisation and preparation of SAARC meetings at the levels of Standing Committee, Council of Ministers and the summit and such other meetings as directed by the Standing Committee. The Secretary General shall attend those meetings or nominate a member of his professional staff to do so;
5. Submit the Annual Budget of the Secretariat to the Standing Committee for approval of the Council of Ministers;
6. Act as the custodian of all SAARC documents and publications,
7. Report periodically to the Standing Committee; and
8. Perform such other functions as the Standing Committee and Council of Ministers may assign.

The first Secretary General Abdul Ashan has sought to initiate a debate on the role, power and functions of the Secretariat and the Secretary General of the forum. In his report to the SAARC Foreign Secretaries, Ashan said it was felt that the responsibility could be 'discharged effectively' if the Secretariat was 'involved' one way or another in all process starting from taking decisions about a programme to its implementation. The Secretary General emphasised that they were "at the disposal" of the member states in "whichever manner they wish to utilise our services" towards strengthening the organisation and making its activities more effective and purposeful. The Secretariat is the only mechanism available full time to the member states exclusively for the work of the organisation. Ashan said its functionalities were committed to "neutrality" and to a SAARC perspective and outlook on all matters.[5] India sees no contradiction between the co-ordinating role of the technical committees, the programming committee and the Standing Committee on the one hand and that of the Secretariat on the other. Each technical committee is responsible for the co-ordination of activities within the sector of its jurisdiction. The Secretariat on the other hand, is responsible for the overall co-ordination of the integrated programme of action.

The professional staff of the Secretariat shall be appointed by the Secretary General upon the nomination by member states. Art. 6(2) says that each member states shall nominate one officer at the level of

Director, who on appointment shall take charge of a Division/Divisions to be assigned by the Secretary General. The appointment of a Director shall be for three years [Art. VI (3)]. In special circumstances the Secretary General may, in consultation with the member state concerned, extend the tenure for a period not exceeding another full term. A Director shall be of the rank of Councellor [Art. VI (4)]. The Director shall perform such functions as may be assigned to them by the Secretary General. The Secretary General shall employ such General Services staff as are necessary for the normal functioning of the Secretariat. The General Services staff shall be nationals of the member states recruited through open competition after adverstisement and shall be appointed by the Secretary General.

The salaries and allowances of the Secretary General and Professional and General Serives staff of the Secretariat shall be determined by the Council of Ministers. The Secretariat, the Secretary General and members of the Professional staff of the Secretariat shall enjoy such privileges and immunities as are admissible to diplomatic missions/envoys and as detailed in the Headquarters Agreement to be reached between the Secretariat and the host country. Other SAARC states will take steps to accord immunities and privileges to the Secretary General and other members of the Professional staff when visiting their territories on official duties consistent with local laws and practices.

As the Art. XI. (2) of the Memorandum, the Annual Budget of the Secretariat shall contain two main components:

(i) Capital expenditure, including all capital costs on such items as procurement of machines, equipment and vehicles, and

(ii) Recurrent expenditure, including all expenses associated with the running of the Secretariat during the Budget year including payment of salaries, allowance and perquisites of all secretarial personnel, utility charges, office requisites and stationery, minor maintenance and any other regular expenses.

Annual Budget of the Secretariat shall be shared by member states on the basis of a formula agreed upon by the Council of Ministers. The accounts of the Secretariat shall be audited annually by a panel of auditors comprising three qualified members nominated by three member states by rotation and appointed every year for a contract period of three weeks by the Standing Committee. The report of the Panel of Auditors along with the annual accounts shall be submitted to the Standing Committee for approval of the Council of Ministers.

The ticklish issue of funding the Secretariat was settled as a result of a twin formula based on constant and variabale contribution. India agreed to pay 32 per cent of the total expenses ($ 400,000 for the first year), Pakistan 23 per cent, Nepal, Bangladesh and Sri Lanka 11 per cent each and Bhutan and Maldives 5 per cent each. The formula had taken into account the capacity to pay as also the imperative of providing a sense of participation to the members.[6]

The signing of the memorandum of understanding regarding the setting up in Kathmandu of the permanent Secretariat for the SAARC induced optimism that the spirit of sharing and joint striving would become a corporate habit with the member countries.[7] Specific institutional measures such as the establishment of the regional centre on meteorological research in India and an agricultural information centre in Bangladesh apart from the regional documentation centre and data bank for Economic, scientific and technical information may well provide the spring board for economic co-operation.[8]

Funding Modalities

In the case of finance, it was decided that contribution by member countries would be voluntary. Certain guidelines were prepared for the reference of the technical committee for making recommendations for the apportionment of the cost for implementing the programmes proposed by it. Following are the guidelines:

(i) Except to the extent otherwise agreed, the cost of travel and subsistence for participants in seminars, workshops and training and other programmes shall be met by their respective Governments and cost of organising seminars, workshops and training and other programmes may be met by the host country or apportioned among participants in proportion to the facilities availed of or financed from external sources.

(ii) Except to the extent otherwise agreed, the cost of subsistence for experts shall be met by the receiving countries and the cost of travel and/or salary of the experts may be paid for by the sending countries, or shared among participating countries or financed from external sources.

(iii) Other costs, including the cost of preparation of studies, shall be shared on a mutually agreed basis.

(iv) In the case of long term projects, the technical committee concerned shall submit recommendations to the standing committee on the modalities for meeting the costs.

(v) In the case of projects and programmes for which sufficient financial resources cannot be mobilised within the region, recourse may be had to external assistance from appropriate sources, with the approval of the standing committee.[9] This would invite unnecessary and unwanted pressures upon the participating countries from the external sources. Thus, it is necessary that financial arrangements must be on strong grounds. A common fund should be established and contributions to the fund should be based on some agreed principles taking into consideration the financial capacity of each member country.

Areas Identified for Co-operation

The Foreign Secretaries in their first meeting at Colombo (April 21-23, 1981) agreed that there were several areas in which mutually beneficial co-operation could take place. The Bangladesh working paper, which formed the basic document on the basis of which discussions were held at Colombo, identified "after a careful analysis of the activities of the existing forums, both regional and international"[10] five areas of co-operation. As a first step it was agreed to set up five study groups with a co-ordiantor country for each in the fields listed below:

1. Agriculture -- Bangladesh (Co-ordinator country)
2. Rural Development -- Sri Lanka do
3. Telecommunication -- Pakistan do
4. Meteorology -- India do
5. Health and Population activities -- Nepal

At Colombo it was decided that the study groups were to conduct indepth studies and make recommendations to the next meeting of the Foreign Secretaries. A committee of the whole comprising senior officials of the seven countries identity and report on other areas of possible co-operation was set up under the Chairmanship of Sri Lanka. The Committee on the whole was only a consultative body and it was for the Foreign Secretaries to take decisions on the conclusions in accordance with the principles adopted by them.

The Foreign Secretaries at their second meeting held in Kathmandu from November 2 to 4, 1981, discussed and endorsed the recommendations of the five study groups. As part of establishing appropriate modalities for implemenation of the recommendations, the study groups were converted into working groups in each of the five areas of co-operation already identified. It was decided to rotate the chairmanship of the working group periodically. It was also agreed that the major task of each working group would be to draw comprehensive programme of action for co-operation in both immediate and long-term phases. The immediate action programme included three components:

(a) Exchange of data and information.

(b) Exchange of experts, training facilities and scholarships.

(c) Organisation of seminars, and workshops on a regional basis.

The long-term programme comprised the following:

(a)assessment of needs and resources,

(b) preparation of specific projects of regional nature, and

(c)modalities for financing the projects.

The most significant development in this meeting was that three additional areas of co-operation were approved:

(1) Transport, (2) Postal Servies, and (3) Scientific and Technical Co-operation.

Maldives, Bhutan and Pakistan respectively were assigned the duty of co-ordination.

It should also be noted that it was decided to promote co-operation among the official national planning organisations of the countries of the region and agreed to initiate action with a view to discussing the matter in greater depth. Further, the Foreign Secretaries agreed to hold their next meeting within six to eight months to consider the implementation of their agreed discussion on regional co-operation. They also agreed to recommend their Ministers to convene a meeting at their level in 1982.[11]

Here mention should also be made to the first meeting of the Committee of the whole from August 31 to September 2, 1981, in Colombo. The Foreign Secretaries in their first meeting in Colombo agreed to set up a Committee of the whole comprising senior officials of the Seven countries to identify and report on other areas of possible co-operation for consideration at their next meeting. It was decided that Sri Lanka would be the co-ordinator country for this meeting. The terms of reference for the committee of the whole in the Joint Communique issued at the conclusion of the Foreign Secretaries' meeting in April were "to identify and report on other areas of possible co-operation for consideration."

The Committee held wide ranging discussions on all aspects of the matter using the Sri Lanka working paper circulated by Bangladesh. The Committee had also referred to the note submitted by Government of India regarding further areas of co-operation. Having considered the substantial economic and social benefits that the member countries can mutually derived from regional co-operation in various fields, and taking note of the views expressed by the representatives, the following thirteen areas of possible cooperation were identified for consideration by the Foreign Secretaries. They are: (1) Education and training, (2) Cultural exchanges, (3) Scientific and technological co-operation including co-operation in the field of New and Renewable sources of energy, (4) Tourism, (5) Transport, (6) Shipping, (7) Monetary co-operation, (8) Co-operation in International Economic Negotiations and Negotiations with multinational co-operation, (9) Information and Mass Communication, (10) Environment including Marine Pollution Control, (11) Postal Services (as part of policies on manpower export, and (13) Promotion of co-operation amongst Regional Planners, Non-Governmental organisations, Academic Research and other institutions.

Keeping in view of the lack of political will the Foreign Secretaries could agree only to three areas from among the thirteen identified by the first meeting of the Committee of the whole. What could be regarded as a great significance was that despite the fact of Pakistani hesitatión, the Foreign Secretaries could move a little ahead by instituting study groups in three areas.

In the third meeting (Islamabad August 7-9, 1982) the Foreign Secretaries considered the report of the study groups on Transport, Postal Services and Scientific and Technological co-operation. They noted with satisfaction that the study groups had completed the task of investigating the scope and feasibility of initiating regional co-operation in their respective areas and unanimously endorsed the recommendations contained in these reports. Study Groups in these three areas were, converted into working groups. They further considered the reports of the working groups on Agriculture, Rural Development, Telecommunications, Meteorology and Health and Population activities and endorsed their recommendations on programmes of co-operation.

The Foreign Secretaries agreed that the implementations of the recommendations of the five Working Groups should be initiated as expeditiously as possible, where the expenditure for such programmes could be met from available financial resources. They agreed to rotate the Chairmanship of the working groups in alphabetical order and term was fixed as two years. On the basis of the agreement arrived at Kathmandu with regard to the promotion of co-operation among the official national planning organisations of the countries of the region, the Foreign Secretaries recommended the holding of a meeting of representatives of the respective national planning organisations of the Seven countries at an appropriate level in New Delhi, prior to the next meeting of the Foreign Secretaries. They also agreed to hold regular consultations by representatives of the countries of the region on matters of common interest relating to international economic issues. It was decided to constitute a study group on sports, arts and culture and the committees of the whole was entrusted with the duty of nominating the co-ordinator for this study group.

While inaugurating the third meeting of the Secretariat, Foreign Minster of Paksitan Sahabzada Yakub Kahan expressed satisfaction over the progress already made in identifying the scope of regional co-operation in various agreed areas. He stressed the need for a deliberate and measured pace to enable to consolidate the gains of each stage before proceeding to the next. He also stressed the need for ensuring an equitable distribution of the benefits of co-operation among all the countries of the region and said that "in our attempts to forge closer economic relations between ourselves, we must ensure that our co-operation benefits not merely the more developed states alone, but each state individually."[12]

India had, meanwhile suggested several areas for co-operation, of which particular significance was its offer to share its experience in oceanography. Countries of South Asian region share the waters of the Arabian Sea, the Bay of Bengal and the Indian Ocean both within and beyond the limits of their national jurisdiction. India said at the meeting that it would be happy to share its experience concerning the use of the sea within the limits of its national jurisdiction with other countries of the region on the basis of reciprocity.[13] India was also stressing co-operation in trade. It had told the other delegations that it should be possible to consider at least limited co-operation among state trading agencies and co-operation in the marketing and processing of commodities of interest.

India urged for greater co-operation in Trade, NIEO, Tourism, Culture, Sports and Games and supported the proposal for regional seminars and workshops, exchange of data and so on. Pakistan was still harping on the political and security atmosphere in South Asia.

The Dhaka meeting of the Secretaries (March 20-23, 1983) fully endorsed the recommendations contained in the reports of the committee of the whole. Here it would be useful to make a mention of the work done by the committee of the whole, assisted by Chairman of the eight working groups, which met in Colombo from January 10-13, 1983 under the Chairmanship of Sri Lanka. The meeting of the committee of the whole arose out of the need to prepare adequately for the ministerial level meeting scheduled to be held in 1983. The Integrated Programme of Action as designed by the Committee of the whole included two broad categories of co-operative activities. These broad categories identified by the working groups included activities amenable to short-term co-operation and long-term co-operation—

(a) Activities amenable to short-term co-operation included *inter alia:*

(i) exchange of data, (ii) exchange of expert services, (iii) training and research, (iv) holding of seminars/workshops in the countries of the South Asian region.

(b) Activities amenable to long-term co-operation included *inter alia*:

(i) establishment of regional institutions for training and research, (ii) creation/strengthening of linkages among existing national institutions in the Seven South Asian countries in the agreed areas of co-operation, (iii) strengthening infra-structural support in such areas as postal services, telecommunications, railways, highways, investment by the participating countries.[14]

Further, the report defined modalities for its implementation at the sectoral level by the Technical Committee and its co-ordination and monitoring at the regional level by the Standing Committee as well as elaborate guidelines and arrangements for its financing.

At the sectoral level, the eight working groups with co-ordinator as Chairman would implement and monitor the Programme of Action in various areas. It was intended that focal points be identified in various Ministries/national institutions/apex organisations, where this had not already been done. At the national level focal points had already been established in the respective Ministries of Foreign Affairs of the Seven countries for overall co-ordination and monitoring.

The Secretaries also decided to recommend the adoption of the integrated Programme of Action by their Foreign Ministers at their meeting which would formally launch its implementation. The Foreign Secretaries decided that the Committee proposed for co-ordinating and monitoring the Integrated Programme of Action at the regional level should be designated as the Standing Committee and be constituted at the ministerial level. They further agreed that the Standing Committee would meet at least once a year and as often as it deemed necessary. The Foreign Secretaries could also call for convening of expert level meetings whenever the discussions of technical issues might warrant. Considering that South Asian Regional Co-operation is an evolutionary process, they further agreed that studies be initiated in due course to identify additional areas of co-operation. The Foreign Secretaries agreed to recommend to their Foreign Secretaries to convene a meeting at the ministerial level between the last week of July and the first week of August, 1983, in New Delhi with a view to launching the Integrated Programme of Action. The Foreign Secretaries noted with satisfaction the report of the meeting of the representatives of national planning organisations of Seven countries,[15] held in New Delhi from January 24-25, 1983 and agreed that it would be useful to hold such meetings periodically. They welcomed the offers of assistance received from the European Economic Community (EEC) and International Telecommunication Union (ITU) for activities connected with regional co-operation in South Asia.[16]

The meeting was convened primarily to prepare the ground to the forthcoming ministerial meeting and the atmosphere in general was smooth. Bangladesh seemed to be the enthusiastic advocate of regional co-operation and called for collective approach to external pressures. The Indian stand was that bilateral cleavages should not be considered as constraints to regional co-operation. The Foreign Secretary of India stated that "the type of regional co-operation we have in mind is neither inward looking nor exclusive. In fact, co-operation within our region on the one hand, and co-operation with other countries and regions on the other could proceed in a manner which would reinforce, rather than obstruct or inhibit each other."[17] It should be noted that the Pakistani attitude was also positive though they were seen half-hearted about a meeting at the political level.

The first meeting of the Foreign Ministers held in New Delhi (August 2, 1983), noted that considerable work had been done at the technical level to identify possible areas of co-operation and prepare specific programmes in agreed areas. It also noted the Committee of the whole at its meeting held at Colombo and the Foreign Secretaries in their meetings held at Dhaka and New Delhi had drawn up an integrated Programme of Action based on the work done at the technical level. The meeting considered the recommendations of the Foreign Secretaries and decided to launch the integrated Programme of Action for South Asian Co-operation, as recommended by them in the areas of Agriculture, Rural Development, Meteorology, Tele-communication, Scientific and Technological Co-operation, Health and Population activities, Transport, Postal Services and Sports, Arts and Culture. The meeting re-affirmed that it would be beneficial to continue co-operation among the National Planning Organisations and academic institutions of countries of the region.

The Foreign Ministers of the member countries of SAARC held their second meeting in Male on July 10-11, 1984. In between Delhi meeting and Male meeting of Foreign Ministers, the Standing Committee met twice, the first session was in New Delhi (February 27-28, 1984) and the second in Male (7-8 July, 1984) on the eve of the Male meeting of Foreign Ministers. The Male session of the Standing Committee prepared the report to be presented to the Foreign Ministers meeting.

At its first session held in New Delhi on 27-28 February, 1984, the Standing Committee considered the reports of Technical Committees. The background note submitted to that session of the Standing Committee reviewed the progress in the implementation of the integrated Programme of Action and put forward some suggestions on the specific issues referred to the Standing Committee as well as with regard to the future work.

The Standing Committee expressed its deep appreciation to the Technical Committees for the work accomplished by them and took note of the reports of the Technical Committees. It expressed its warm gratitude to the Chairman of the Committees and to the countries concerned for organising the meeting approved by the recommendations contained in the reports. It also took decisions on the specific issues referred to it by the Technical Committees as well as with regard to the future work of the Technical Committees. As already noted, the Standing Committee held its second session in Male (7-8 July, 1984) to prepare for the second meeting of Foreign Ministers of South Asian countries, 10-11 July, 1984. It noted with satisfaction that the interim period between its first and second sessions marked an active phase in the actual implementation of the programme undertaken by the nine Technical Committees. The Standing Committee expressed regret at the lack of response from industrialised nations in meeting the concern of developing countries facing serious loss of development momentum.

The report in paticular noted with regret that despite the strong pleas from developing nations, it had not yet proved possible to augment the resources available for the International Development Association (IDA). The Committee expressed "great disappointment" over the continuing imphase in North-South dialogue and with "serious concern" the significant erosion in multilateral co-operation. In this context, it noted with "deep regret" that no appreciable progress was made in meeting the concern of developing countries at the London Summit of industrialised countries despite approaches made by various leaders from non-aligned and developing countries to convey their concern. The Committee ended its meeting after approving the draft report to be presented to the Foreign Ministers' meeting commencing at Male on July 10, 1984. The meeting noted with satisfaction the reports submitted by the Standing Committee following its first and second sessions in New Delhi (from 27-29 February, 1984) and in Male (from 7-8 July, 1984) respectively. They considered and endorsed the recommendations of the Standing Committee.

Thus at the first instance eleven areas were identified and the integrated Programme of Action was launched. When the Association traversed from the first Summit in Dhaka (1985) to the third one in Kathmandu (1987), it was decided to take up following subjects: (1) problem of terrorism, (2) drug trafficking and abuse, (3) women in development, (4) child welfare, (5) food security reserve, (6) audio-visual exchange, (7) expanded tourism on the basis of limited convertibility of the national currencies, (8) educational exchanges at the University level, (9) documentation centre, (10) youth volunteer programme.

Implications for development of a SAARC Community

Even a cursory look at the SAARC co-operation would reveal the fact that SAARC co-operation still revolves round peripheral items of co-operation. The SAARC activities since the Dhaka Summit consisted of the meetings of Technical Committees on the nine subjects agreed for co-operation. The progress made so far had been confined to preparation of compendia and indices in regard to the capacities of the South Asian Countries in different fields, celebration of events like SAARC games, film festival and archaeological conference. It had been decided to set up two regional centres in India and Bangladesh on meteorological research and on agricultural information. The most notable success has been achieved in regard to international economic issues, as the conclusion reached at the ministerial meetings in Islamabad became the basis of the stand taken by the developing countries at GATT discussions.

Tangible regional co-operation which impacts beneficially on the lives of people everywhere must involve not thousands but millions of South Asian citizens. Programmes and events should be devised to raise people's consciousness of their identity as South Asian sports is a ready medium for mass participation as the sports events in Kathmandu and Dhaka have already testified.

India repeatedly at several SAARC meetings suggested that the area of activity should be expanded to include core areas of co-operation like trade, industry, energy money and finance. India maintained the view that it was very difficult to ignore these sectors which carried the potentiality to contribute to the economic development of the region. India desired that SAARC would be able to take in the very logical step of forging links of co-operation in these sectors also. In fact, India had made this suggestion at the first Summit in Dhaka and reaffirmed it more than once subsequently.

The reaction of others on the theme of including core economic areas in the list of SAARC activities, varied with Bangladesh welcoming the idea and Pakistan lukewarm to it. Bangladesh went with India as its Foreign Secretary Fakhruddin Ahmed said that the conceptual framework of the co-operation among the SAARC countries would have to materialise in the "specific projects and action programmes" which could ultimately prove beneficial to the peoples of the member countries. "In order to be able to generate concrete benefits, SAARC should gradually and increasingly encompass core areas of economic activity." According to him, Bangladesh has a "very open mind" in this regard. He said any suggestion for new areas of co-operation should be seriously examined to facilitate its eventual inclusion in the programme of action.[18] Besides Bangladesh for generating and prompting multi-sectoral investment in production, infrastructure and technology build up on South Asia. Dwelling the idea of the investment institution, he explained that the institution could be a joint enterprise with equity of participation of the public and private sectors of the member states.

Pakistan, on the other hand, wanted to consolidate the progress made so far on the agreed areas of co-operation, with emphasis and priority as time bound programmes of action. Pakistan is of the opinion that multiplicity of ideas for co-operation without follow-up measures is counter-productive. Programmes should, therefore, be realistically framed.[19] At the same time Pakistan expressed concern at the state of the global economy and said that the developmental efforts of the Third World countries continued to be impeded by an increasingly hostile environment. The prices of commodities, which constituted a major source of export earnings, had fallen down to alarming levels. The debt burden continued to grow to the detriment of the socio-economic progress in the third world. Relying on the latest figures, he said the total external debt of the developing countries was close to $ 1,000 billions, nearly twice the value of their total exports of goods and services. The situation, he said, called for concerted action to create greater trade opportunities for the developing countries and enhanced transfer of resources on soft terms.

India, perceptively reacted to the consolidation theme of Pakistan and called on the South Asian nations to go beyond mere consolidation of regional co-operation. "Consolidation is important, but not enough. There must also be "expansion and growth" Rajiv Gandhi said while opening the meeting of the Council of Ministers of the SAARC, in New Delhi.

Sri Lanka was not against broadening of activities to include core economic areas under the SAARC framework. Jayawardene said: "We have to expand and enlarge our activities. We will have to enter important areas as trade and commerce. The growth of our association will depend on the growth of mutual trust and confidence."[20] Bangladesh supported India's suggestion that the co-operation should now gradually expand to cover some core areas of economic activity. Ershad asserted: "A carefully planned expansion of our co-operation to encompass such core area should contribute objectives that we have set for ourselves."[21] Bhutan boldly accepted the idea and said the SAARC countries should extend their co-operation to the vital field of trade and joint economic ventures in the region. It should devote less time to workshops and seminars and concentrate more on concrete regional projects. King Wangchuk said: "The goals we set for ourselves must be realistic and time-bound."

As already noted India's persistent effort to bring core economic sectors such as trade, industry, energy, environment, within the scope of SAARC, remained unsuccessful. As was seen the strongest protest to it came from the Pakistani side. The inclusion of these areas would help ensure equalisation of benefits among the member countries. Co-operation in some of these areas would bring real benefits to the people of the region within a short span of time. Apprehensions that co-operation in these fields would adversely affect the broader interests of the smaller countries of the region were unfounded propaganda, from the Indian point of view. Another important aspect of co-operation under the SAARC framework should be noted. It is afflicted by the malaise of adding more and more proposals to its inventory of unfulfilled good intentions. Aside from the setting up of its Secretariat at Kathmandu in January, 1987, and the incredible number of meetings and seminars exceeding 500 on a wide range of concerns shared by the member countries, the work of SAARC till date can hardly be equated with the task of converting the logic of collective self-reliance into a culture of planned interdependence. It should also be mentioned that the meetings of the SAARC have not generated among its members the degree of enthusiasm that has marked other regional groupings of the same variety. The informal bilateral discussions the heads of state and Government hold during the summits are regarded of greater value than the main conference itself. The reason for this relatively low key approach lies partly in the fact that the political and strategic perceptions of the members do not converge in the manner of those participating in the ASEAN.[22] Obviously, the other members are still to get over their fears that the Indian economy would take on a dominant role and are also unwilling to dilute the special relationship they have developed with other powers. Though the achievement of SAARC is rather modest in tangible terms, no one can deny the fact that SAARC had already made a beginning in forging a distinct South Asian identity and collective approach to common problems. However, the present set of institutions, SAARC has established, are not strong enough to incorporate future requirements.

A brief discussion of bilateral issues and external factor influence would throw much light into the underlying factors that keep SAARC away from co-operation and integration in core economic areas including trade, industry and finance, that a regional organisations of this type ought really to set as its main goal. Chapter V and VI look at the bilateral and external relations in South Asia, since these relations hold the key to the regional co-operation potentials in SAARC region.

Notes

1. Andrew Axline, *op. cit.*, p. 32.
2. Joint Communique issued at the conclusion of First Meeting of Foreign Secretaries (Colombo – April 21-23, 1981), issued by Conference Cell, Ministry of External Affairs, New Delhi.
3. *Indian Express*, 10 August, 1982.
4. *The Hindu*, 10 August, 1982.
5. *Economic Times*, 31 October, 1987.
6. *The Hindu,* 16 November, 1986.
7. *Ibid.,* 18 November, 1986.
8. SAARC Charter.
9. Extracts from the Bangladesh working paper of November 1980, issued by Conference Cell, Ministry of External Affairs, New Delhi.
10. Joint Communique issued at the conclusion of the second meeting of Foreign Secretaries, Kathmandu, November 2-4, 1981.
11. Text of the inaugural address of Sahabzada Yaqub Khan, Foreign Minister of Pakistan, Islamabad, August 7, 1982.
12. India has been conducting surveys for the past few years for utilising living and non-living and non-living marine resources. It had also succeeded in lifting polymetalic nodules from the Indian Ocean bed and has also organised a research expedition to Antarctica.

13. Report of the meetings of the Committee of the whole (Colombo, January 10-13, 1983).
14. The deliberations at the meeting were devoted to three main themes, namely: (a) national planning models and extension of planning techniques to social accounting matrix; (b) organisation and implementation of social and anti-poverty programmes; and (c) impact of world economic situation and outlook on national development performance and prospects.
15. Joint Communique issued at conclusion of Fourth Meeting of Foreign Secretaries (Dhaka, March 25-30, 1983).
16. Text of the Statement by M. Rasagotra, Foreign Secretary of India at the Fourth Meeting, Dhaka, March 28-30, 1983.
17. *The Hindu* (Madurai), 14 November, 1986.
18. *Ibid.*
19. Text of the Bangalore address.
20. *The Hindu*, 17 November, 1986.
21. *Ibid.*
22. *Ibid.*, 24 June, 1987.

CHAPTER V

BILATERAL POLITICAL ISSUES AND REGIONAL CO-OPERATION

This chapter examines the political aspects of co-operation in its bilateral context which may set the stage for other forms of co-operation including both larger multilateral co-operation in political as well as economic field.

Although the SAARC Charter or its forerunner the New Delhi Declaration did not say anything definitely about 'Political co-operation' reference was made to the following in the opening paragraph of the Charter: ''Desirous of pormoting peace, stability, unity and progress in the region through strict adherence to the principles of the UN Charter and non-alignment, particularly respect for the principles of sovereign equality, territorial integrity, national independence, non-use of force and non-interference in the internal affairs of other states and peaceful settlement of all disputes.''[1]

Besides, the second paragraph of the Charter mentioned the importance of achieving peace, freedom, social justice and economic prosperity in South Asia by ''fostering mutual understanding, good neighbourly relations and meaningful co-operation among the member states which are bound by ties of history and culture.''[2]

It further referred to the need for joint action and enhanced co-operation to protect the interests and aspirations of the people of South Asia. An awareness of the common problems convinced that regional co-operation among the countries of South Asia is ''mututally beneficial, desirable and necessary for promoting the welfare and improving the quality of the life of the peoples of the region.''[3] The Charter recognised that increased co-operation, contacts and exchanges among the countries of the region ''will contribute to the promotion of friendship and understanding among their peoples.'' Also one of the objectives of the Association is to contribute to mutual trust, understanding and appreciation of one another's problems and to strengthen co-operation among themselves in international forums on matters of common interest.[4]

The Charter also laid down the basic principles of co-operation within the framework of the association: (a) Respect for the principles of Sovereign equality, territorial integrity, political independence, non-interference in the internal affairs of other states and mutual benefit, (b) such co-operation shall not be a substitute for bilateral co-operation but shall complement them, and (c) such co-operation shall not be inconsistent with bilateral and multilateral obligations. At the same time the Charter provided that "decisions at all levels shall be taken on the basis of unanimity" and "bilateral and contentious issues shall be excluded from the deliberations".

Thus regional peace and stability and productive bilaterialism are the important themes of this chapter. Any study of peace and stability in South Asia has to take into account the behaviour of India or what others perceive as the behaviour of India. The neighbours very much feel the self-awareness of India's pre-eminence and India's quest to assert itself in the affairs of the region. Every Indian neighbour, except perhaps Bhutan and Maldives, is involved, at least, in one dispute with India, like sharing of river waters, fencing the border, ethnic-religious conflicts, territorial dispute, nuclear policy or the desire to get declared a zone of peace, involvement in one another's internal problems to mention a few. Each state in South Asia perceives a threat to its territorial integrity from their big neigbour in the region. The fear of Indian dominance keeps them away from cultivating closer bonds based on common historical and cultural homogeneity. Smaller South Asian states felt that they are "confronted with an India which is imperial in outlook and difficult to persuade."[5] It is true that India has problems with all its neighbours in South Asia but that is because India alone shares land or maritime borders with other states in the sub-continent. The "core geographic location and ethnic religious pluralism"[6] made India the common factor in any study of inter-state relations in South Asia. The dispute that marred India's relationship with Pakistan are different from its difficulties with Nepal or Bangladesh or Sri Lanka. This fact needs to be recognised while making an analysis of the nature, trends and shifts in bilateral relations in South Asia. What should be borne in mind in this context is that the success or failure of regional co-operation in the region depends on the positive or negative nature of India's bilateral interaction with Pakistan, Sri Lanka, Bangladesh and Nepal. There exists no major difficulties in India's bilateral relations with Bhutan and Maldives.

Peace and security in South Asia can perhaps be studied within the framework of the concept of 'security community' developed by Karl Deutsch. According to Deutsch there are two types of communities *viz.*, amalgamated and pluralistic. Amalgamated security community is very difficult to attain. In such communities the goal of integration is not only the preservation of peace among the participating units but also the attainment of common role identity and greater power intended to specific and general purposes or an amalgamation of all these with a common Government. Deutsch enumerated twelve social and economic background conditions which seems necessary for the successful attainment of an amalgamated security community.[7]

Since SAARC has no desire for forging amalgamated community the conditions that favour pluralistic security community only needed to be considered. According to Deutsch three conditions are important for this type of community:

1. Compatability of major political values.
2. Capacity of the Government and politically relevant strata of the participating countries to respond to one another's messages, needs and actions quickly, adequately and without resort to violence.
3. Mutual predictability of the relevant aspects of one another's political, economic and social behaviour (but these relevant aspects are far fewer in the case of a pluralistic security community than they would be in its much more tightly knit amalgamated counterpart).

Deutsch considers that Pluralistic security communities are easier to establish and to maintain and hence an important and effective means to keep peace among the participating members. The process of establishing pluralistic security requires following background conditions for its success:[8]

1. An increasing unattractiveness and improbability of war among the political units of the emerging pluralistic security community, as perceived by their Governments, elites and (eventually) populations.
2. Spread of intellectual movements and traditions favouring integration, and preparing the political climate for it.
3. Development and practice of habits and skills of mutual attention, communication and responsiveness, so as to make possible the preservation of autonomy and substantial sovereignty of the participating units and preservation of stable expectations of peace and peaceful change among them.

J.S. Nye has criticised the concept of security community. He considers this concept as the earliest and most intriguing from a value point of view. At the same time it is the most difficult one to measure. It is also "difficult to develop a scale of security community rather than merely describing its pressence of absence."[9] Despite these difficulties, "the concept of security-community is important and goes to the heart of our concern" observes Nye.[10]

South Asia has been a conflict prone region right from the days of independence. Hindu-Muslim communalism with its far-flung ramifications, Bangladesh migration, sharing of waters of common rivers, disputes involving Tin Bigha and New More Islands, barbed wire-fencing of the Indo-Bangladesh borders, demarcation of maritime boundary, Chakma refugee problem, Tamil tensions and the problem of Nepali Ethnics in India and Indians in Nepal are the sources of bilateral conflicts in South Asia. The discussions of some of these issues would help to understand the political situation in South Asia and to explore the possibilities of a security community in the Deutschian framework or a modified form. In relation to peace and security in South Asia, one important factor needs to be mentioned. As noted by Leo Rose and Satish Kumar "one fact little noted outside the region is that all of the South Asian states except Pakistan have already been brought within the matrix of an Indian security system which is regional rather than national in scope. In some cases, this is through formal agreements; in others through the unilateral extension of the Indian system to neighbouring States."[11] Obviously only Pakistan posed a challenge to the Indian doctrine of regional security. Thus the major hurdle to this "united but rather unique form of regional security system" has been Indo-Pak relations.

India and Pakistan are the traditional rivals in the region. So the heart of the question of regional co-operation is the question of Indo-Pak understanding. The relation between India and Pakistan are "the key-stone for South Asian co-operation of any kind"[12] and the relations between these two countries suffer from the "crucial dichotomy of unmitigated personal warmth and undivided national suspicion and animosity."[13] A fundamental and long-term improvement in relations between these two countries are to be achieved for the viability of regional co-operation in South Asia. What is required is a reconciliation of the basic contradictions with regard to political values, political frameworks, international perceptions and attitude.[14]

In relation to the points mentioned above, political issues in South

Asia as it appeared in the SAARC forum will be briefly presented in the hope that it might give valuable insights into the process of productive bilateralism, peace and regional stability.

Dhaka Summit

The first ever summit of the South Asian heads of state and Government clearly brought out the attempt, by the neighbouring countries except perhaps Maldives, to isolate and pressurise India. The manner in which Srilankan President Jayawardene praised Prime Minister Rajiv Gandhi and India is a case in point. He turned to Rajiv Gandhi and praised him as the chosen leader of India and said, ''On Rajiv Gandhi we rest our hopes, he must not fail us. He cannot, our duty is to help him to the utmost. He should tell us what each of us should do and we must respond as best we can.'' About India he said: ''India the largest in every way larger than all the rest of us combined can by deeds and words create the confidence among us so necessary to make a beginning.'' Similarly General Zia-Ul-Haq praised India and Rajiv. During the course of his address he departed from the prepared text of the speech and mentioned the consensus arrived at between himself and Jayawardene in the informal discussions on the eve of the summit.[15]

Significantly on the eve of the summit, a Bangladesh daily carried an interview with General Zia. In this interview he listed various commonalities among the Seven states and added: ''There is more than one factor that is common to all. There has been only one aspect and that is the India factor. India with whom we would like to join hands and be in the mainstream and play that much of a role which can generate confidence rather than fear for smaller neighbours. But unfortunately, it is only India which has some sort of dispute with every country.''[16] He viewed the size of India as an inhibiting factor, ''Through SAARC we hope to convince India that it must take measures to play its part as the centre figure in South Asia but with the recognition that there is nobody big or small. They are equal, independent and autonomous states. India must also realise that it is the smaller states which have the greater ego. It won't cost India to play low profile and generate confidence in others. Let India buy something from small countries and only in this way we can live in peaceful co-existence.[17]

Another irritant was the stamp episode. It was decided to release commemorative stamps to mark the launching of SAARC. When all were set for the function and copies were distributed among the delegates the Indian officials found that the Pakistani stamp showed Jammu and

Kashmir as a separate territory. Likewise Maldivian stamp showed Sikkim as a separate territory. Both were objectionable to India and so the function was given up. While Maldives issued an explanation stating that the stamp design was based on a map of a U.N. agency, no such explanation came from Pakistan. Through the stamp episode General Zia cleverly brought to the fore the bilateral dispute between India and Pakistan by the back door.

The king of Bhutan was seemingly objective but some of his remarks were double-edged. He said, "It may neither be possible nor desirable to limit discussions in our meetings to issues of a non-political nature, for the political climate of our region will undoubtedly cast a long shadow over our deliberations. In the geographical realities of our region it would be unrealistic to ignore the primacy of the political factor, as in the final analysis it will be the political environment of the region which will determine the shape and scope of regional co-operation in South Asia." Ragiv Gandhi viewed regional co-operation in a different way. To him the regional framework would not demand reshaping of foreign policies of the member countries. In his address at the inaugural plenary he asserted, "Certainly we have problems and difficulties and these do impose constraints on us. Enduring co-operation is co-operation adapted to the realities of our condition. The model we have evolved for ourselves is a model which is in accord with our realities, our compulsions and our genius. We have not sought to melt our bilateral relationships into a common regional identity, but rather to fit South Asian co-operation into our respective foreign policies as an additional dimension." The Prime Minister elaborated this point further by adding a few words on the modalities and mechanisms evolved for the SAARC framework.

The summit provided opportunities to discuss the bilateral issues informally. Thus Rajiv Gandhi met Zia-ul-Haq, General Ershad and President Jayawardene separately to discuss bilateral problems.

This informal consultations were fruitful to a very large extent. General Zia told Rajiv Gandhi that he would allow Khan Abdul Ghafar Khan to attend the Congress centenary celebrations in Bombay later that month. As promised, the Pakistan Government allowed Ghafar Khan to visit India. His Government also provided a plane to bring him to New Delhi. As a follow up, Pakistan President visited New Delhi on December 17, 1985 generating great optimism about future Indo-Pak relations. The two leaders declared that the two countries would not attack each other's nuclear installations. It is thus clear that Dhaka has brought about greater personal relationship among the leaders.

Bangalore Summit

The Bangalore Summit was significantly different from that of the first in the sense that there was no collective effort to corner India. The highlight of the summit was the informal consultations between Prime Minister Rajiv Gandhi and President Jayawardene to sort out the Tamil ethnic issue. Another aspect of the Bangalore summit was the high political drama enacted by the Pakistani delegation including Prime Minister Mohammad Khan Junejo at the summit venue.

Rajiv Gandhi inaugurated the summit and stated that SAARC would not be a political association. Referring to bilateral relations he said: "Bilateral relations have their difficult moments. SAARC reminds us that at such moments we should seek what unites us and not what divides. We have consciously decided not to burden SAARC with our bilateral concerns." The Bangalore summit, however, was clouded by tensions between the region's two larger powers. India accused the Pakistan authorities of aiding Sikh separatism in its Punjab state and of developing a nuclear bomb. For its part Pakistan was concerned about a build up of Indian troops along the Indo-Pakistan border. In his talks with Rajiv Gandhi, Prime Minister Junejo denied reports that his country tested a triggering mechanism for a nuclear Bomb. But Gandhi told the reporters: "To be honest, we are not utterly convinced."[18] The bilateral squabble was brought up by Junejo in his speech referring to the troop movements: "We in South Asia should agree to notify one another's significant troop movements. We could agree also to invite observers when the movements exceed in agreed threshold." He said Pakistan was deeply opposed to nuclear weapons and fully backed a proposal by Nepal to declare the region a nuclear-free zone. He then referred to 300 million Muslims in South Asia and gave a peace of advice to Rajiv Gandhi to follow the admirable example of Bangladesh President Ershad who had visited other countries of the region during his tenure as Chairman of SAARC. Turning to Rajiv Gandhi, Junejo said, President Ershad had set a fine example. "A good example needs to be followed. We recommend it for your consideration, Mr. Chairman."[19]

The informal bilateral contact between Rajiv and Junejo did not arouse much enthusiasm. In fact it was far from cordial. That was because both sides failed to prepare the ground for the talks. Pakistan Foreign Secretary Abdul Sattar initiated a diplomatic offensive against India at the SAARC media centre on several issues hampering normalisation of relations between the two states. Sattar asserted that the principle of bilateralism did not exist in the Simla agreement. It could be seen that distorted facts to suit his arguments. Both the timing and the content of his remarks drew widespread attention and invited sharp reaction from the Indian side. At his press conference Rajiv Gandhi took a tough line and asserted that any new dialogue have to take into account three factors:

1. Islamabad's nuclear ambitions;
2. Its role in instigating terrorists operating in Punjab and Kashmir; and
3. The issue of drug trafficking.

At the same time Prime Minister Rajiv Gandhi and Srilankan President Jayawardene held discussions in a cordial atmosphere with the Srilankan side stressing that it wanted India to continue its good offices. Jayawardene's arrival some three hours ahead of the others made it possible for the two leaders to exchange their views at the airport itself. Rajiv Gandhi and Jayawardene met three times during the summit intervals. Related to this intensive consultations between Rajiv and Jayawardene, LTTE leaders Prabhakaran, Balasingham, and Tilakan were flown to Bangalore by a special IAF plane for urgent consultations for a political forum but it has started exercising a subtle influence on political relations in South Asia in the senses that it has facilitated a personal relationship between the South Asian leaders. The nature and content of co-operation among the member countries will be determined by the political realities in the region. This was clearly evident in Bangalore as well.[20]

Air-Lift Operation: Aftermath

In the wake of India's air-lift SAARC forum was subjected to the litmus test. The biggest exercise during the inter-summit period, the meeting of the foreign ministers of the member countries had acquired significance in the context of relief supplies in Jaffna and the reaction of other SAARC countries to that action. India's airlifting of food materials to the Jaffna Peninsula was widely condemned in South Asia. For instance Pakistan expressed "great concern" over the air space violation of Srilanka and stated "clearly, such intrusion into the air space of an independent state constituted a deplorable infringement of international law. This regretable action militated against the prospects and promotion of confidence, co-operation and good neighbourly relations in South Asian region."[21]

Bangladesh Foreign Secretary stated that the ethnic problem in Srilanka was the internal affair of the island and added that "negotiated and peaceful" settlement of the issue would diffuse the tension.[22] The air dropping mission had evoked sharp resentment from the political circles in Bangladesh. Political parties in that country viewed the "penetration into the Srilankan space" by the Indian airforce plane as a deliberate and gross violation of international rules but also an act of outrage upon Srilankan sovereignty. They also termed this operation as a direct threat to the people in other small states in the South Asian sub-continent. The central committee of the five party alliance observed that India had set an "undesirable and unwanted instance by unauthorised airdropping of relief materials to the Tamil separatists.[23] Nepal and Maldives also condemned the Indian action. A Foreign Ministry spokesman said Nepal deplored the Indian intervention and would always condemn such violations of sovereignty and condemned the act as a violation of Srilanka's integrity.[24]

Maldives considered the act as a grave development. President Gayoom described the violation of Srilanka air space by India as "a grave, grave development" between India and Srilanka."

Some uncertainty developed in regard to the scheduled meeting of SAARC council because of doubts over Srilanka's participation. It is worth mentioning here that the neighbours kept far from cashing in on India's possible discomfiture at the Srilankan boycott of the SAARC meeting. On the other hand they seemed anxious to stave off any such embarrassment.[25] It is evident that they wanted to keep SAARC alive. Obviously the Foreign Ministers of Pakistan, Bangladesh, Maldives and Nepal in individual communications said they were perturbed over the reported statements that Srilanka might keep away from the SAARC and urged Colombo to participate fully in the SAARC session in New Delhi.[26]

Indicative of the premium placed on the forum of SAARC by these countries was a communication from the Pakistan Foreign Minister Yakub Khan to his Srilankan counterpart Hameed: "Unfortunate differences have arisen on the eve of a highly important meeting of SAARC which has made noteworthy progress." In the judgement of Pakistan, "It is of the utmost importance that nothing should happen that should constitute a setback to the consolidation of SAARC." Pakistan was "disturbed by some reports" that Srilankan Government might not participate fully, the message said.[27]

At last, on 13 June 1987 Srilanka formally informed the Indian Government that its Foreign Minister would take part in the meeting of the SAARC Council. Simultaneously the Srilankan Government announced its decision through a press release in Colombo. Hameed had informed his counterparts in Pakistan, Bangladesh, Nepal and Maldives about it while appreciating their concern over Srilanka's participation in the SAARC meeting. A Foreign Ministry release said: ''Immediately after the decision (to participate) was taken, the Minister of Foreign Affairs, A.C. Shahul Hameed sent the following message to the Foreign Ministers of Bangladesh, Maldives, Nepal and Pakistan : "I thank you for your message. We deeply appreciate your concerns. Sri lanka has given the most careful consideration to them and will participate in the forthcoming SAARC ministerial meeting. It is our fervent hope that this joint efforts of South Asian countries in building co-operation and strengthening goodwill and peace in our region will take a step forward at the New Delhi meeting. I thank you and your Government for the understanding and respect you have extended to Srilanka. It is our firm view that mutual respect, mutual understanding and mutual accommodation which constitute the very core of peaceful co-existence should continue to be the cornerstone of our regional endeavour.''[28]

However the Srilankan delegation avoided India's hospitality. The Srilankan Foreign Secreatary, W.T. Jayasinghe, did not attend the dinner hosted by K.P.S. Menon, for the visiting colleagues. The Sri Lankan delegation told the management of the Ashoka Hotel where they were staying that the Bills for their expenses would be paid by their High Commission in New Delhi.[29]

New Delhi meet of the SAARC Council – 18-19 June 1987

At the council meeting participants conveyed their views obliquely through cautiously worded formulations. For instance, the favourite themes of the Pakistani delegation were norms for good neighbourly relations and indispensibility of respect for interantional principles. The meeting clearly confirmed growing nexus between Srilanka and Pakistan against India. India had taken note of the visit of Srilankan National Security Minister Lalith Athulath Mudali to Islamabad and his talks there. After arriving in Delhi Hameed had informal consultations with Foreign Ministers of Maldives, Nepal and Bhutan. Srilankan stand was that it could seek military assistance from whichever country it desired, to curb the activities of Tamil militants. It gave the example of Nordic Council, some of whose members belonged to NATO and others were neutral on the East-West issues. None of these affiliations had stood in the way of their regional co-operation.

As expected Hameed made a fervent plea for evolving a new mechanism, where at every meeting at the Foreign Ministers level we have informal closed-door meetings where could air our views candidly." He underscored: "SAARC must not end up as a deaf, dumb and blind association. What I am saying is that as we grow, we must face new challenges, new situations, new developments. I believe solutions to problems have to be found and worked out from within." While "in our wisdom we had thought that it would be prudent to avoid speaking of bilateral issues ... making such a rule sacrosanct, in the long-run could spell disaster", he asserted. Hameed specifically raised three issues that could affect the smooth conduct of SAARC and said ways and means of overcoming them must be found. The issues were transborder terrorism, cross-border ethnic and religious affinity and differing perceptions of foreign policies. He spoke of ethnic, religious affinities among communities and warned against "cross-border involvements". Such involvements could seriously affect bilateral relations and undermine the SAARC spirit. "If any religious ethnic group in a country has a problem, it should settle it within the framework of its national boundary, without the involvement of any other country in the region on the basis of religious or ethnic commonality."

Tacit support to the Srilankan Government's position on the Indian action of air dropping of relief materials could also be discerned in the speeches of the Foreign Ministers of Pakistan, Bangladesh and Nepal. The Foreign Minister of Bangladesh Humayun Rashid Choudhury made the specific point that SAARC Charter provided for strict adherence to the principles of U.N. Charter and non-alignment, particularly respect for the principles of sovereign equality, territorial integrity, national independence, non-use of force and non-interference in the internal affairs of other states and peaceful settlement of all disputes and added: "Herein lies our strength and the key to the success of our common endeavour in quest for co-operation, peace and progress, prosperity and stability of our region." The Pakistan Foreign Minister Shahabzada, Yakub Khan, urged that "the use of force, or the threat of use of force should have no place amongst us." He referred to a cynicism within and outside SAARC countries that differences in South Asia were "too strong to permit the fruition of regional co-operation amongst us." These observations were obviously intended to indirectly indict India for the air space violation of Srilanka.

Srilanka, strongly supported by Pakistan called for a change in the basic concept of the Association so as to provide for a discussion and possible moves for settlement of bilateral problems. India's airdropping mission was not specified even by Srilanka and Pakistan although it seemed very large in the discussions. The Srilankan Foreign Minister devoted his entire speech to formulations based on Colombo's perception of the Indian action. As against the total backing from the Pakistan Foreign Minister Yakub Khan, Sri Lanka got the muted support of Bangladesh's Humayun Rasheed Choudhury and Nepal's Shailendra Kumar Upadhyaya. Bangladesh and Nepal drew attention to SAARC's Charter and the need to strictly adhere to its principles of sovereign equality and territorial integrity among others. Bhutan and Maldives did not mention that. They chose not to involve themselves in these controversies.

India's opposition to SAARC taking up bilateral and contentious issues was made clear by External Affairs Minister N.D. Tiwari, at the very outset. In polite but categorical terms he told his colleagues from South Asia and relations between neighbours could not be wholly free from problems and therefore co-operation under SAARC was based on the primacy of "our common concerns" over individual differences. "We should not seek to drive full advantage from whatever unites us. Ours is an effort to widen the area of agreement and co-operation in spite of bilateral differences." That was why a conscious decision had been taken not to burden SAARC with bilateral concerns. Otherwise "we will end up in a stalemate and miss the immense opportunities that regional co-operation offers." He explained the Indian position thus: "Co-operation under SAARC is predicted on the premise that our common concerns should be considered more important than our individual differences. We should seek to derive full advantage from whatever unites us. Ours is an effort to widen the area of agreement and co-operation in spite of bilateral differences. That is precisely the reason why we took a conscious decision not to burden SAARC, with our bilateral concerns. For we realised that by doing so we will end up in a stalemate and miss the immense opportunities that regional co-operation offers." It is thus clear that India firmly rejected the suggestion that the forum of SAARC be used for sorting out bilateral problems. India maintained the view that SAARC had been set up to promote co-operation in technical, economic and social fields in South Asia on the basis of unanimity and the inclusion of bilateral controversies in its scope would impose unbearable burdens on the grouping. Thus bilateral issues just could not be raised in SAARC.

Kathmandu Summit

The meeting between Rajiv Gandhi and Jayawardene had become the political highlight of the Kathmandu Summit. The Srilankan leader added to the interest of the event by announcing his intention to discuss with Rajiv Gandhi the draft of a treaty on defence and foreign policy. Thus Srilanka recognised India's security interest in the region. Both the leaders conferred on ways to restore peace in the troubled island. They met for two hours after dinner in the first night and again met for another round in the second night. It was reported that they also discussed the proposed defence and foreign relations treaty between the two countries. The Minister of State for External Affairs Natwar Singh (India) and Minister for Land Development Gamini Dissananyaka (Srilanka) were also present at the talks. Natwar Singh had two meetings with Foreign Minister A.C.S. Hameed at the summit venue. However the talks specially related to the situation on the ground in Jaffna, the reservations of the Tamil Groups, on the draft bills relating to the powers of the provincial council and preparing the political ground for holding of elections.[30]

Rajiv Gandhi and King Birendra held talks on bilateral issues on the day. Gandhi and Wangchuk held a breakfast meeting on the second day. Bilateral issues were reviewed at the meeting.[31]

India and Pakistan had two rounds of ministerial level discussions on normalisation of bilateral relations. Rajiv Gandhi and Junejo discussed a wide range of bilateral matters and agreed to accelerate the dialogue on outstanding issues. The two Prime Ministers decided to hold an early meeting of the secretaries for economic affairs of the two countries to discuss the promotion of economic co-operation and increasing trade. The Prime Ministers also agreed to hold an early meeting of the secretaries for interior and home affairs for taking suitable measures to prevent the illegal crossing of borders by unauthorised persons. The defence secretaries of the two countries were also asked to hold their third meeting to discuss the Siachin glacier issue. It was further decided that the Surveyor Generals of the two countries should meet to demarcate the international boundaries at the Sir Creek close to the Rann of Kutch. The maritime boundaries would be settled in accordance with the international law covering the sea lines.[32]

Rajiv Gandhi and Ershad met in Kathmandu on 3 November 1987 and agreed to start discussions at tripartite level to augment water flows of the common rivers. They also reached an understanding on Secretary level meeting to discuss water resources development. During the meeting the two leaders discussed the entire gamut of relations including unresolved issues. Rajiv Gandhi informed Ershad about the process of completion of handing over of the Tin Bigha corridors to Bangladesh. He said the process of completion of administrative and legal formalities for handing over the corridor to Bangladesh was in the final stage.[33]

Obviously the dominant theme of the speeches at the inaugural session was peace and co-operation and the leaders hailed in this context the prospect of a treaty between the Soviet Union and the U.S. on nuclear arms reduction. They hoped it would lead to reduction of nuclear arms stockpiles and save the world from the threat of nuclear holocaust. The Indo-Srilanka agreement came in for special praise as a notable event with the objective of promoting peace and stability in the region. In his address Rajiv Gandhi called upon South Asian countries to have greater mutual interaction as their economies are likely to be better sustained through regional co-operation. He said "we have forged a regional grid of relationship" that was breaking the barriers that had kept them apart. "We have succeeded in nurturing South Asian Regional Co-operation because it is firmly grounded in the realities of the region." He asserted that "ours is a concord for co-operation, not a concourse for controversy." SAARC's method of work made it a democracy of sovereign equals. With the clear vision of the outgoing chairman Rajiv Gandhi noted that SAARC was taking shape as "a factor in determining our place in the world" and the regional understanding among the member countries was "a positive political development". Their relationship was "breaking the barriers that have kept us apart and South-Asian co-operation is gradually "entering our collective consciousness.

Srilankan President spelt out in detail how the peace accord between India and Srilanka had significance for the whole of the region. "Success of SAARC or not will have to depend on the extent to which we can confront and solve bilateral problems we may have between us." "Srilanka's separatist problem", he added further, "provides a convincing illustration in support of the generalised observations that have been made," by signing the Indo-Srilanka agreement in settling this separatist problem." And at the same time, "we have established the basis for the conduct of our foreign relations on the principles that nothing would be done by either, that could be detrimental to the other in any way." This, he said has to be "regarded as an unexceptionable principle and indeed a prerequisite for good neighbourly relations." It would contribute to the stability of the region.

Bangladesh President Ershad said pointedly, 'we cannot, of course, deviate from our commitments enshrined in our charter, particularly the respect for principles of sovereign equality, territorial integrity, national independence, non-use of force.''[34] He noted that political issues at the bilateral level had been purposefully kept out of the SAARC agenda for co-operation but ''we have certainly, albeit informally addressed issues that are of concern to us, internationally, regionally and even bilaterally.'' Bangladesh welcomed the peace accord India and Srilanka signed to end the ethnic conflict in the Island state. Any development that would further the cause of peace is welcomed by Bangladesh. President Ershad proposed a plan for multipurpose Himalayan water resources development aimed at turning the Himalayan resources into the lifeline of the regional development efforts. He said the plan would cover such areas as flood control, irrigation, navigation, hydro-electric power generation, municipal and industrial water supply, fish and wild life protection, recreation and water quality.[35]

The President of Maldives Abdul Gayoom, noted that although bilateral relations did not come under the banner of SAARC it was sure that ''every one of us is happy to note the new understanding reached between the two brotherly countries as a result of the accord.'' He paid growing tributes to the Indo-Srilankan accord and said he saluted the political wisdom of both President Jayawardene and Prime Minister Rajiv Gandhi in arriving at a very difficult solution to a four year old ethnic problem.

The King of Bhutan, Jigme Singye Wangchuk, said that the most notable event in South Asia during the tenure of Rajiv Gandhi as Chairman of SAARC was the Indo-Srilanka Agreement. ''By bringing about the peace accord Prime Minister Rajiv Gandhi and President Jayawardene have demonstrated their deep devotion to the spirit of SAARC and its noble objective of promoting peace and stability in our region.'' He described the accord as a high spirit of SAARC co-operation. He voiced deep concern over the ever expanding nuclear arsenal and called upon the two super powers to work resolutely towards global disarmament.

Pakistan again raised the issue of keeping the South Asian region free of nuclear weapons and called for a regional agreement placing a comprehensive ban on nuclear tests. Addressing the inaugural sessions of the SAARC summit in Kathmandu Prime Minister Junejo said a joint renunciation of the nuclear option as a binding insturment would reassure their peoples. None of the countries had said it intended to produce nuclear weapons and, therefore, an agreement on the subject was inherently achievable. Junejo suggested that the SAARC secretariat be authorised to establish contact with the ASEAN secretariat and discuss modalities by which the two regional groupings could benefit from each other's experiences.

Surprisingly enough the King of Bhutan supported this view. In his address King Jigme Singye Wangchuk said he wanted to "express serious concern at the prospect of neclear weapons development in South Asia. We must take a united stand against this ominous trend. We can hardly call upon the major powers to curtail their nuclear weapons programme if we ourselves are not prepared to prevent its development in our own region. In my view, SAARC can provide a forum to conduct a meaningful dialogue among our countries on this vital issue."

Pakistan referred to the contentious issues and suggested a collective agreement renouncing the nuclear weapons and barring the entry of these weapons into the region. Pakistan raised the nuclear non-proliferation at every summit knowing well that such security related matters "just as bilateral matters," are not supposed to be taken up at the regional forum. India, as usual, strongly resisted successfully the induction of any such paragraph into the draft declaration. Since India does not consider the nuclear non-proliferation issue to be a regional one, Pakistan raised the issue repeatedly. Zain Noorani, Pakistan's Minister of State for Foreign Affairs said that Pakistan was willing to adhere to a regional nuclear non-proliferation arrangement and it invited constructive consideration of the proposed SAARC forum. The high drama enacted in the media centre at the summit venue by a Pakistani delegate over the Afghan plea for SAARC membership is worth-mentioning. A visibly agitated Pakistani delegate to the SAARC summit in Kathmandu stormed into the media centre carrying Indo-Pakistan tensions behind the scene into the open. What prompted the Pakistani `background' briefing was a conference decision in the wake of Afghan's application for joining the SAARC. The Pakistani sources was at pains to contradict an impression that the SAARC decision to examine admission of new members was a victory for India. Ironically it was Pakistan which made a reference to the Afghanistan's application for admission into SAARC and said it would support the application only when Kabul "recovers its sovereignty and independence". Pakistan having brought up the subject, India promptly took it up in informal consultations at which Natwar Singh, Minister of State for External Affairs, rebutted the Pakistani insinuation that Afghanistan was not a sovereign independent nation to be eligible for SAARC membership. Nepali spokesman of the conference made a cryptic announcement that SAARC foreign secretaries would examine the question of admission of new members and grant observer status in the association. Indian sources confirmed they had indeed taken up the Afghan request in informal-ministerial level consultation. On the contrary Pakistani sources claimed the Afghan plea was 'rejected' by the ministers and none of the other members had endorsed the Indian support to Kabul.[36]

Obviously India thwarted a bid by Pakistan to write into the draft declaration of SAARC summit in Kathmandu a reference to military balance and call for regional security and nuclear non-proliferation in South Asia. The draft declaration was finalised by high officials of SAARC member states. At the instance of India, Pakistan withdrew its amendment on keeping the region as a nuclear-free zone.

The Heads of State and Government apparently spent a lot of time discussing a suggestion from Bhutan that the Kathmandu declaration contain a paragraph welcoming the steps taken by India and Srilanka to end strife in the Island. The conclusions of this discussion evolved in stages. At first, doubt was expressed whether bilateral issues could be commented upon in the SAARC declaration. Then it was decided in the affirmative. Then comes the question of discussing Indo-Srilanka Agreement. It was decided to discuss the question. But, when it came to considering Bhutan's suggestion, Pakistan began opposing such an idea on the ground that it was a situation similar to Afghanistan, where troops were occupying a foreign country. The idea of having a paragraph in the declaration on the Agreement was then dropped. But, evidently what remained from all the polemics over Bhutan's suggestions was the conclusion that bilateral issues could be commented upon in the SAARC declaration.

Islamabad Summit

Highlights of the Islamabad summit can be summarised as follows:

1. The Islamabad declaration recognised the need for stronger economic co-operation. It could incorporate this idea as the basis for intensified co-operation, as a result of two favourable developments:

   a. A new climate had been created by the unilateral declaration of Prime Minister Rajiv Gandhi, that India would not attempt to secure any undue and unfair advantages from its SAARC partners. This bold initiative was received warmly by all other partners. President Jayawardene praised Rajiv Gandhi for making such a bold statement.

b. Another reason for the new willingness to admit the idea of economic co-operation was unleashed by the positive change in the attitude of Pakistan to the idea of increased economic co-operation. They toned down the resistance to economic interaction under the new democratic leadership. While addressing the concluding session Benazir Bhutto said: "I believe that the study being carried out in the area of trade, manufacture and services will lend itself to enchanced economic exchanges and will lead to harmonisation of our economic efforts towards the socio-economic progress of our people."

2. At the initiative of Pakistan, education was included in the list of SAARC activities. As articulated by Pakistan, the Heads of State and Governments decided to declare 1989 the "SAARC year for combating Drug Abuse and Trafficking" and to initiate efforts for co-operation in this area. The Pakistani offer to institute a centre for Human Resources Development was also accepted.

3. Islamabad summit approved a perspective SAARC-2000 regional plan to pool their resources to provide the basic needs of the people in the region. The concept places emphasis on the human dimension in development planning by focusing attention on meeting basic human needs such as food, primary health care, literacy and shelter. Following are the salient features of the perspective SAARC- 2000 regional plan:

   a. A vision of a long term growth of the SAARC region as a whole on the basis of growing regional complementalities, interdependence and collective self-reliance.

   b. Expansion of regional co-operation in core economic areas, trade, industry, money, finance and joint ventures.

   c. Initiating long-term measures to minimise the adverse effects of changes in the international economic environment

   d. Each member country establish a focal point in its Planning Commission or relevant ministry for the purpose of consolidating sectoral studies organised under the aegis of SAARC for bringing them under a long-term perspective.

However the main SAARC show has been sidelined by the bilateral talks between Rajiv Gandhi and Benazir Bhutto. With an earnest desire to work towards a new phase of relationship, both the Prime Ministers exchanged views on the bilateral issues. The emphasis in the Indian diplomatic approach, that there could be no discussion on confidence-building measueres until Pakistan abandoned its covert support to terrorism in Punjab, has undergone a significant shift. As a result three agreements, on the basis of the directions given by the two Prime Ministers, were signed:

1. An agreement on the prohibition of attack against nuclear installations and facilities of both the countries;
2. A cultural co-operation agreement; and
3. An agreement on the avoidence of double taxation of income from international air transport.

While the first two were signed by the Foreign Secretaries of the two countries, the third one was signed by the Ambassador of India in Pakistan and his counterpart in India.

The non-attack of nuclear facilities agreement commits both the countries to "refrain from undertaking, encouraging or participating in directly or indirectly, any action aimed at causing the destruction of or damage to any nuclear installation or facility in the other country."[37] Under the agreement each country is obliged to "inform the other on January 1 of each Calender year of the latitude and longitude of its nuclear installations and facilities and whenever there is any change."

Benazir Bhutto summarised the significance of the signing of the three agreements at a Press conference jointly addressed with Rajiv Gandhi. She said that, "the momentum for peace had begun" after sixteen years and that is symbolic of the "sincere desire of the Prime Minister of India and of mine to remove all differences and to bring an era of peace.... It is our endeavour to work to reduce tensions between our two countries."[38]

Rajiv Gandhi stated at the Press conference that the Siachin issue and the Pakistani encouragement of terrorism in Punjab had been discussed at the official level. It is worth mentioning here that Benazir Bhutto has categorically stated that her country would not use the Sikh card against India any more.

As stated by Benazir Bhutto the Islamabad Summit had given a fresh momentum to the process of mutual co-operation. She said: "It is my sincere hope that the excellent personal relations that we have been able to establish with each other will be crucial in building bridges and increasing a better climate of mutual understanding among our nations."

It is very clear that the changes in the international environment unleashed by the positive elements of the bold initiatives of the Soviet President have paved the way for friendliness between the traditional rivals in South Asia. Rajiv Gandhi, the first Indian Prime Minister to pay an official visit to Pakistan in 28 years, was received warmly by the Pakistani Prime Minister and the bilateral parleys between them proved beyond any doubt the potentialities of SAARC summit as a confidence building mechanism. At the same time, no one can pass by the blackspot at the otherwise beautiful face of the Islamabad exercise, the other leaders were virtually neglected. The King of Nepal and the President of Bangladesh expressed their resentment against this by eulogizing the late President Zia-ul-Haq. Obviously this was not to the liking of both India and Pakistan on account of the fact that they were engaged in a process of theorising the dawn of democracy in Pakistan right from the inaugural plenary to the concluding ceremony of the Islamabad Summit.

In the preceding pages an attempt has been made to examine the presence or absence of the three conditions – compatibility of major values, capacity to respond to one another's need, mutual predictability of political economic and social behaviours–required for constructing a pluralistic security community. When studied within the rubric of the distinct pattern of issues and interactions in SAARC region, variations are discernible in each of the conditions, from issue to issue and country to country. At the same time all the members share a common concern with regard to tensions and conflicts in the region. Regional peace has been a favourite theme of the leaders of the South Asian Seven. The noticeable feature of bilateral interactions in the region at present is the induction of positive elements in the bilateral relations between India and Pakistan in the sense that mutual consultations and exchanges with a desire to forge mutual understanding have increased ever since the inauguration of the SAARC dialogue. A sense of community has already started developing among the partners with features of mutual predictability of behaviour. However it is not possible to construct a scale to measure it mathematically.

Admittedly the process of community formation in South Asia is markedly different from the Deutschian model presented at the beginning for the reason that in the SAARC region there is not a desire to get politically unified. On the other hand all the partner countries aspire to keep and further the individual identity while participating in the multilateral framework. The aspiration is to attain developmental objectives through the regional framework without sacrificing political independence.

However, it can safely be stated that SAARC sessions, especially the summits have definitely developed into a structure of grievance articulation though not yet a full-fledged confidence building mechanism.

Notes

1. SAARC Charter, published by the External Publicity Division, Ministry of External Affairs, New Delhi.
2. *Ibid.*
3. *Ibid.*
4. *Ibid.*
5. Hamid H. Krilbash, "Security Concerns of South Asian States", *Regional Studies Series*, No. 3, Spring 1985, p. 114.
6. Partha S. Ghosh, "Ethnic and Religious Conflicts in South Asia", *Conflict Studies*, No. 178, p. 2.
7. (1) Mutual compatability of the main values relevant for political behaviour; (2) A distinctive and attractive way of life; (3) Expectations of stronger and rewarding economic ties or joint rewards; (4) A marked increase in the political and administrative capabilities of at least some of the participating units; (5) Superior economic growth of at least some participating units (as compared to neighbouring territories outside the area of prospective integration); (6) Some substantial unbroken links of social communication across the mutual boundaries of the territories to be integrated, and across the barriers of some of the major social strata within them; (7) A broadening of the political elite within at least some political units, and for the emerging larger community as a whole; (8) Relatively high geographic and social mobility of persons, at least among the politically relevant strata; (9) Multiplicity of the scope of the flow of mutual communications and transactions: (10) Some overall compensation of rewards in the flows of communications and transactions among the units to be integrated; (11) A significant frequency of some interchange in group roles (such as being in a majority or a minority) among the political units ; and (12) Considerable mutual predictability of behaviour. See for details Karl W. Deutsch, *The Analysis of International Relations* (Prentice Hall, 1968), pp. 193-96.
8. *Ibid.*, p. 21.
9. J.S. Nye, *Peace in Parts* (Boston, 1971), p. 48.
10. *Ibid.*, p. 48.
11. Leo E. Rose and Satish Kumar, "South Asia" in Werner J. Feld and Gavin Boyd eds., *Comparative Regional Systems* (New York 1986), p. 264.
12. Rishikesh Shaha, "Guidelines from experience", in Pran Chopra ed., *Future of South Asia* (New Delhi), 1986, p. 165.
13. Satish Kumar, "Pakistan", *World Focus* (New Delhi), Vol. 6, No. 11-12, November 1985, p. 53.
14. Asia Week, Vol. 12, No. 48, 30 November 1986, p. 46.
15. *Bangladesh Observer*, 6 Dec. 1985.
16. *Ibid.*
17. *Hindustan Times*, 16 Nov. 1986.

18. On the eve of the summit Tamil Nadu Police arrested several militant leaders including V. Prabhakaran and Balasingham. Their cadres were also taken into custody and released after questioning. It was significant that the operation took place on the eve of the summit, when Srilankan President was scheduled to discuss the situation on the island and the prospects of a negotiated political settlement with the Prime Minister of India.
19. L.K. Sharma, ''SAARC spirit bobs despite disputes'', *The Times of India* (Bombay), 20 November, 1986.
20. *Pakistan Times*, 5 June, 1987.
21. *Bangladesh Times*, 5 June, 1987.
22. *POT*, Bangladesh Series, 9 June, 1987.
23. *Mainichi Daily*, 9 June, 1987.
24. *Bangladesh Times*, 10 June, 1987.
25. *The Hindu* (Madurai), 13 June, 1987.
26. *The Hindu* (Madurai), 17 June, 1987.
27. *The Hindu*, 14 June 1987, *Times of India* (Delhi), 14 June, 1987.
28. *The Hindu*, 18 June, 1987.
29. *The Hindu*, 4 November, 1987.
30. *Hindustan Times*, 4 November. 1987.
31. *Dawn*, 5 November, 1987.
32. *Bangladesh Observer*, 4 November , 1987.
33. *The Hindu*, 3 November, 1987.
34. *POT*, Bangladesh Series, 4 November, 1987.
35. *Times of India* (Delhi), 1 November, 1987.
36. *Hindustan Times*, 3 November, 1987.
37. According to the agreement ''the nuclear installation or facility includes nuclear power and research reactors, fuel fabrication, uranium enrichment, isotopes separation and reprocessing of facilities as well as any other installations with fresh or irradiated nuclear fuel and materials in any form and establishments strong significant quantities of radioactive materials.''
38. *The Hindu* (Madurai), 1 January, 1989.

CHAPTER VI

COMMUNITY FORMATION IN SAARC'S EXTERNAL RELATIONS: LESSONS FROM ASEAN

The political objective of the third world countries enganged in regional co-operation is to change the socio-political, economic conditions of their people and to redress the unequal nature of their relationship with the developed countries. Third world integration schemes and co-operative systems "assign considerable importance to the manner in which the overall external environment can affect integration through the formation of trade, investment and aid links between a given system and a third party or parties in the developed world."[1] It is incontestable that there is an integral connection between politics and economics and it is erroneous to approach economic affairs in isolation from politics. As noted by the Colombo non-aligned summit, a complete change of political attitude and demonstration of a new political will is an indispensable prerequisite for the realisation of the New International Economic Order. For the same collective bargaining *vis-a-vis* the external actor or actors, particularly the developed `North' is a basic requirement and co-ordination of external policy is the first step in this direction. Only then can dependency to a few centres of the developed North be progressively reduced. Through harmonisation of external policy, regional co-operative system can limit to the minimum the negative influences of strings attached to trade, aid and investment flows. Thus regional approach to development for collective self-reliance should take into account the lessons in the North-South dialogue inaugurated in 1975 and the recommendations of the Brand Commission which emphasised the interdependence of the developed and developing nations.

The countries of the third world have been "struggling to gain equality of opportunity in their development, and to be their own masters, not only politically but also economically and culturally."[2] Besides the countries of the South are making "efforts to increase their share in the international production of goods and in the world trade. And they plead for beneficial co-operation, assistance and transfer of resources, financial grants, low-interest loans, foods and technologies – in order to overcome their poverty and achieve equality of opportunity.''[3]

In the broader canvas of North-South dialogue and South-South co-operation harmonisation of external relations should be given top priority. In other words, it would be appropriate to give less emphasis to the internal integrative aspect and more attention to co-operative relations of South Asian Countries *vis-a-vis* the external actors.

As stated by Mytelka, ''there is a logical need to regulate direct foreign investment and technology transfer within regional integrative system so as to create the conditions necessary for the accomplishment of other integrative goals.''[4] An attempt is made in this chapter to examine the possibilities of community formation in SAARC's external relations. Accordingly a review of the external environment is made at the outset followed by an analysis of the ASEAN documents to draw lessons from the ASEAN experience in this respect.

External Milieu

South Asia was a region neglected right from the day of the birth of the new states of the sub-continent in the late 40s, by both the super powers because of their deep involvement in the Western theatre. But now the region is inextricably intertwined with the strategic interests of the great powers.[5] Apart from both the super powers, China is also a prominent actor in the politics of the reigon. Thus it is evident that a strategy for peace, security and development in South Asia cannot be designed without taking into account the interests and concerns of the two super powers and China in the region.[6] Ideological and systemic similarity or difference got only a low premium in the shaping of the foreign policy behaviour of these powers because the same was drafted not to suit the ideological image but to satisfy the real politik requirements. The fact is that they are led not by ideological purity but by ''pretentious ideologies''.[7] The super powers involvement and association with the formation and development of regionalism in third world regions have well been explained by S.D. Muni. ''The super power geostrategic doctrines have played a very crucial role in shaping the varying forms of regionalism experiences in the third world both by imitating as well as encouraging them. For instance, in the case of the U.S. from Monroe (1824) to Carter the third world regionalism has received a specific incentive. The Soviet Asian Collective Security plan also sought to promote regional groupings in the third world to suit its strategic interests though this did not have much success.''[8] The most important factor that motivated the big powers to promote third world regionalism is economic. Economically the early and growing capitalism needed to integrate raw material sources as well as markets which eventually resulted in the establishment of colonial powers. The urge for such integration continues even in the post-colonial period. However the advanced capitalism now seeks to bring about regional integration and co-ordination in various third world countries for manufacturing and semi-processing purposes to cushion labour and other pressures at home.[9] The regional factors of extra-regional linkages in South Asia are trade, currency, banking, communication information flows, technology transfers, transport and shipping, flow of financial resources etc. "The extra-regional linkages are sustained by mutually competitive sectors of the various South Asian Countries. The divergent strategies of development in the region particularly the outward-looking nature of almost all of India's neighbours, have further augmented the respective extra-regional linkages."[10]

There are indications that the United States played a crucial role at the initial stage of the efforts towards regional co-operation. For instance, two former national security advisers to American Presidents, Henry Kissinger and Zbigniew Brezenski indicated that the American Government would view the co-operative framework in positive light.[11]

Michael Armacost welcomed South Asian regionalism and stated that "we endorse the process of South Asian regional co-operation and will consider sympathetically any proposals that the South Asians might collectively make to U.S. for assistance on a regional basis.[12] He further stated that the United States would endorse steps such as Sino-Indian border negotiations, which reduce regional tension.[13] President Reagan congratulated the heads of Governments of the Seven countries on their first ever summit in Dhaka for the formal launching of SAARC. President Reagan in a message to the summit Chairman, President Ershad of Bangladesh said the United States "stands ready to provide appropriate assistance at your request in launching programmes of regional co-operation."[14] He congratulated the heads of States and Governments and the people of South Asia and said that the United States from its own experience, down the years, was well aware of the practical benefits which could be achieved from regional co-operation.

The United States renewed its offer to support SAARC nations co-operative efforts aimed at development of the region. This renewed support was made known to the Foreign Ministers of the SAARC countries over a lunch hosted by U.S. Secretary of State George Shultz.

He reiterated the Reagan offer of 1985 December to support SAARC in any way the members themselves think appropriate. He said Washington "applauds" the SAARC efforts. "The South Asian Association for Regional Co-operation is in our judgement a flourishing concern.... Although we do not want to push ourselves on the organisation, we do stand ready to help if the countries of the region so desire."[15]

In July 1980 President Zia-ur-Rehman of Bangladesh visited Beijing and affirmed Bangladesh's commitment to the policy of creation of an environment of enduring peace and stability in South Asian region. The official Chinese media gave wide coverage to President Rehman's visit to China[16] and since then China viewed regional co-operation in South Asia as a positive development for collective self-reliance; and instrument to "safeguard peace and stability"[17] in South Asia and the Gulf and welcomed it warmly. The official newspaper *Renmin Ribao* appreciated greatly the meeting of the Foreign Secretaries in Kathmandu in November, 1981:

> Facts prove that if there is sincerity and consultations are held on the basis of quality, tolerance and understanding, co-operation on the basis of mutual repect for each other's sovereignty and mutual benefit can be enhanced. Regional co-operation has just begun..... it will contribute to the peace and stability of South Asia and the rest of Asia.[18]

In August 1983, a people's Daily commentary hailed the Foreign Ministers meeting, which added political thrust to the process of regionalism in South Asia, as "a contribution to regional stability and economic development in the Seven South Asian nations." The commentary described this as being "completely in the interests of the people of the Seven countries to develop friendly co-operation on the basis of equality and mutual benefit" and this was the correct path to travel in the direction of collective self-reliance and economic prosperity."[19] Chinese Premier Zhao Ziyang expressed his warm congratulations and said, "The convening of the summit is an event of great significance in the region which will be conducive to peace in the region." The Premier expressed the hope that the South Asian countries would live in unity and friendship, enhance co-operation to mutual benefit and maintain stability of South Asia and contribute to South Asian co-operation.[20]

After making a careful study of all the aspects, Soviet experts expressed the view that the Bangalore Declaration contained 'important evidence' of the fact that the ideas advanced by Gorbachev at Vladivostock on peace and security in Asia Pacific region can make a real dent. Soviet commentator Olef Kitosanko wrote in Pravda that the joint efforts made by the participants to resolve common problems are ''evidence of the great potentialities of that experience and possibilities to broaden the geographical framework of co-operation to promote world peace and human progress.''[21] This statement is the most positive Soviet response to SAARC so far. During the Rajiv-Gorbachev summit in Moscow in May 1985 the Soviet leader only talked of ''elaborating a general comprehensive approach to the problem of Asian security.''[22] The Soviet approach since then became more comprehensive and concrete as spelled out at Vladivostock by Gorbachev. However, the Soviet Union has been maintaining, since the initiation of the move strong reservation about the nature and future of SAARC due to the generous support of the United States and China and also due to the pro-west proclivities of some of the member countries of the Association. ''It may be kept in mind that the Soviet response to SAARC has been quite formal and restrained. During its formative stages Soviet diplomats have occasionally whispered their apprehensions that SAARC may be goaded into a position where it serves the Western strategic interest in the region.[23]

What has been stated above brings home the fact that the Soviet Union is not quite happy with the South Asian regionalism because it is apprehensive of the overenthusiasm expressed by the United States and China. The Soviet Union is well aware of the U.S. efforts to shape SAARC to suit the latter's geo-strategic interests. The Soviet Union would like the development of autonomous regionalism in South Asia with India being the core component.

SAARC Evolving Approach to External Factors

SAARC has not yet obtained group solidarity to deal collectively with the pressures and challenges coming from extra-regional sources. However South Asian leaders are well aware of the importance of developing a regional culture to respond collectively to outside actors, even though there exists disagreement with regard to the approaches to peace and security in South Asia. For instance the Delhi Declaration on South Asian regional co-operation is ''mindful'' of the Declaration on collective self-reliance among non-aligned and other developing countries adopted at the Seventh Non-aligned Summit held at New Delhi which called upon all countries concerned to mobilise all necessary resources and deploy the requisite means in support of sub-regional, regional and inter-regional co-operation among non-aligned and other developing countries." However this Declaration did not say anything definitely about harmonisation of foreign policies or unified stand in dealing with non-members.

Further, Art. I of the SAARC Charter says that the objective of the Association shall be among other things, "to strengthen co-operation among themselves in international forums on matters of common interests and to co-operate with international and regional organisations with similar aims and purposes."[25] These objectives of the SAARC would go in conformity with the U.N. General Assembly Resolution of 17 December 1971, on Indian Ocean. This resolution wanted to exclude great power rivalries and competition as well as bases conceived in the context of such rivalries and competition from the Indian ocean area.

An analysis of the SAARC documents makes it clear that SAARC countries have demonstrated common concern with regard to the following matters:

1. NIEO and World Trading System through GATT.
2. Multilateral Trade Negotiations.
3. World economic-scene, depressed commodity prices, rising protectionism, global recession, lower export earnings and debt crisis. The Seven countries agreed to consult regularly and co-operate closely in international economic conferences and institutions in order to promote common interest.
4. Commonly held optimistic view regarding the potentialities of the super power summit to contribute to lasting global peace.
5. Concurrence in the matter of comprehensive Test Ban Treaty.
6. Conformity in respect of the utility of the U.N. System.
7. Support to the various activities of the U.N. System.
8. Common resolve to preserve and strengthen the U.N. System.
9. Faith and commitment to the principles and the dynamics of the NAM.

However a close look at the SAARC reveals the evident lack of comprehensive and coherent set of principles which give group identity to SAARC in its external relations. In other words the external domain has not yet been defined in clear cut terms. Nevertheless in the area of economic development co-ordinated actions and approaches are not a difficult affair. Harmonisation of views in the area of economic development would become a major instrument for cultivating common politico-strategic perceptions.

Lessons From ASEAN

ASEAN experience provides valuable lessons with regard to Community formation in external relations. In 1976, at Bali, the Heads of State and Government signed the Treaty of Unity and Co-operation. This treaty and the declaration of concord set forth the guiding principle of political solidarity of ASEAN in its external policy.

According to the Treaty of Unity and Co-operation ASEAN countries desired to enhance peace, friendship and mutual consultation on matters affecting all the members consistent with the spirit and principles of the Charter of the U.N., the ten principles adotped by the Asian-African Conference in Bandung in April 1955, the Declaration of the Association of South-East Asian Nations signed in Bangkok on 8 August 1967 and the Declaration signed in Kuala Lumpur on 27 November 1971. Besides, the Treaty of Unity and Co-operation enumerates a set of fundamental principles which shall guide the member countries relations with one another and relation with countries external to the region :

a. Mutual respect for the independence, sovereingnty, equality, territorial integrity and national identity of all nations;
b. The right of every state to lead its national co-existence free from external interference, subversion or coersion;
c. Non-interference in the internal affairs of one another;
d. Settlement of difference or disputes by peaceful means;
e. Renunciation of the threat or use of force;
f. Effective co-operation among themselves.

Art. 6 of the Treaty provides that in order to accelerate economic growth in the region the ASEAN states shall promote the greater utilisation of their agriculture and industries, the expansion of their trade and the improvement of their economic infrastructure for the mutual benefit of their peoples. In this regard they shall continue to explore all avenues for close and beneficial co-operation with other states as well as international and regional organisations outside the region. In addition to this Art. 9 states that the member nations shall endeavour to foster co-operation in the furtherance of the cause of peace, harmony and stability in the region. To this end the ASEAN states shall "maintain regular contact and consultations with one another on international and regional matters with a view to co-ordinating their views, actions and policies." Besides the Declaration of ASEAN Concord clearly states as an objective of the Association the vigorous development of an "awareness of regional identity" and agreed to exert all efforts to create a "strong community" respected by all, and respecting all nations on the basis of mutually advantageous relationships.[26]

For the attainment of the above-said objectives member nations adopted a programme of action to strengthen "political solidarity by promoting the harmonisation of views, co-ordinating positions and where possible and desirable, taking common actions". Correspondingly they decided to accelerate joint efforts to improve access to markets outside ASEAN for their raw material and finished products by seeking the elimination of all trade barriers in those markets, developing new usage for these products, towards this end the member states pledged to adopt "common approaches and actions in dealing with regional grouping and individual economic powers. Another provision of the Concord states that the "principle of ASEAN co-operation on trade shall also be reflected on a priority basis in joint approaches to international commodity problems such as the reform of international trading system, the reform of international monetary system and transfer of real resources in the United Nations and other relevant multilateral forums, with a view to contributing to the establishment of the New International Economic Order." From the foregoing it is clear that co-ordinated external policy is considered as the important tool for the furtherance of regional solidarity.

Development of regional awareness by means of projecting aspects of commonalities available in history, geography and culture seemed to be the primary requirement in this respect.

In addition to the extensive guideliness included in the Treaty of Unity and Co-operation and the Declaration of Concord following principles were agreed upon to steer ASEAN's extra regional relations:

1. Co-operation with ASEAN as a group should not be at the expense of existing bilateral arrangements.
2. Co-operation should serve to complement ASEAN's capabilities and not supplant them.
3. Co-operation should be for projects conceived by ASEAN which are of a regional character and for the benefit of all ASEAN countries.
4. Co-operation should be unconditional.[27]

Furthermore, complex structures and institutions were set up to carry out the expanding network of collective relations with other countries, regional groupings and international institutions. These would include a large number of committees, study groups meetings and joint consultative groups. The important joint consultative groups which ASEAN established for the conduct of its external relations are the ASEAN-Australia Forum, the Special co-ordinating of ASEAN (SCCAN), the ASEAN Brussels Committee, joint study group for ASEAN-EEC dialogue and ASEAN-Japanese Forum. Similar institutional structures have been established to conduct external affairs with the United States, Canada, New Zealand, the United Nations Development Programme (UNDP), Economic and Social Commission for Asia and the Pacific (ESCAP). The ASEAN Geneva Committee was established to co-ordinate policy relating to multilateral trade and tariff negotiaons in GATT. In addition to this a number of committees were set up to maintain continual communication between World capitals and ASEAN capitals. Member countries' Ambassadors in capitals of the countries concerned were made members of these committees. Thus ASEAN-Washington Committee performs ASEAN's relations with the U.S. and so on. To facilitate efficient and smooth co-ordination of above stated third party relations, a country was designated as co-ordinator for each of the committees as given below:

Indonesia – Japan and the European Communities
Malayasia – Australia and West Asian Countries
Philippines – U.S.A. and Canada
Singapore – New Zealand
Thailand – UNDAP/ESCAP

Apart from the countries and multilateral institutions mentioned above ASEAN is engaged in formal dialogue with India, the South Pacific Bureau of Economic Co-operation (SPEC), Latin American Economic System (SELA) etc. covered by joint approaches in regional and international organisations and third countries would include the following:

1. Liberalisation and improvement of the IMF compensatory financing facility.
2. Commodity policies on items of interest of ASEAN involving natural rubber, timber products, vegetable oil and oilseeds, tin, copper, sugar, and hard fibres.
3 a. Common position on trade issues in the multilateral trade negotiations (MTN).

b. North-South dialogue
c. UNCTAD
d. U.N. General Assembly.
4. Trade co-operation, investment promotion, industrial co-operation, technology transfer, manpower training, stabilisation of export earnings, food production and development co-operation.

From the foregoing it is evident that ASEAN achieved tremendous success in forging unity in the agreed upon areas of external relations. This political solidarity and international visibility could not have been attained but for the high level political commitment. In other words the inauguration of the extra-regioal dialogue is the result of a political push given by the Bali summit of the Heads of Governments in 1976. In fact this summit was a watershed. Admittedly ASEAN got the required political thrust from the similarity of views with regard to national, regional and international political issues. ASEAN was conceived as a multipurpose organisation whose ostensible activities were social and economic co-operation but whose underlying *raison d'etre* lay in political co-ordination to cope with a still threatening regional environment.''[28] Similarly, Adam Malik, former foreign minister of Indonesia stated in October 1974 : ''Although from the outset ASEAN was conceived as an organisation for economic, social and cultural co-operation and although consideration in these fields were no doubt central, it was the fact that there was a convergence in the political outlook of the five prospective member nations.[29] Furthermore all the ASEAN states maintained close political and economic relations with the United States. All but Indonesia had military and strategic linkages with the U.S. or its allies on an anti-communist plank.

Similarly ASEAN received positive support from Japan, Australia and New Zealand also. Later ASEAN obtained approval and support from Soviet Union and China because of the presentation of a unified stance. It is remarkable that ASEAN received expressions of acceptance from the Communist World also. ASEAN attained this recognition as a result of the concrete manifestation of group solidarity *vis-a-vis* third country relations. This ASEAN success can be attributed to the fact that ''Consensus points picked from the rubble of single issues and conflicting interests have with much fanfare been identified as ASEAN principles.''[30] Furthermore they have ''discovered that their being together could be more beneficial to them particularly in dealing with other international organisations and aid-giving agencies.''[31] This discovery is a result of interminable interactions and constant consultations among the member countries. Frequently held mutual consultations contributed to bring together diverse national views to a structure of common views. Obviously ASEAN proved most effective in presenting group solidarity towards outside countries. The most important lessons drawn from the ASEAN experience in respect of community formation can be reduced to three keywords: informality, frequent consultations and patience.[32]

To what extent ASEAN success is applicable to the regional forum in South Asia? The South Asian fabric of multilateral co-operation is fundamentally different from that of ASEAN. As already noted the harmonised external policy of ASEAN is facilitated by the close ideological and political orientation of the ASEAN states. Such a consensus on basic political and ideological values is not available in SAARC region to stabilise and strengthen sketchy emergence of SAARC solidarity.

It would be very difficult to develop the culture of collective approach so far as this region continues to be the theatre of conflict and competition. Intra-regional political issues, tensions and instability are well manipulated by the extra-regional actors in accordance with their global rivalry and competition. For instances the bilateral difference between India and Pakistan have been exploited by Washington to protect their interest mainly in South West Asia. Pakistan has become an agent of the U.S. in this part of the globe. This U.S.-Pakistan strategic consenus has a negative impact all over the region. It did further aggravate the bilateral cleavages between India and Pakistan.' At times the United States tried to develop simultaneous defence relationship with India and Pakistan, two bitter rivals in South Asia, probably encouraged by a similar policy in regard to Turkey and Greece or Israel and Egypt. In the post-Afghan phase there may be a considered move from the part of Washington, to build a military supply arrangement with India. There exists economic, scientific and technological relations between them. The fact is that all the countries in the region are linked to the United States either by politico-strategic relationship or through trade, aid and investment linkages.

Another aspect of U.S. strategy in this region is its support to SAARC. All the states in South Asia view with suspicion the special relationship between India and Sovieet Union. No other country in the region is friendly to Soviet Union. Strategic discord and differences in security perceptions among the regional actors brought the two super powers to the region, to further aggravate the existing cleavages. China is the third non-regional actor influencing regional affairs.

In South Asia the overall external environment is favourable to growth and further consolidation of SAARC because all the prominent external actors welcomed it. Yet the picture is not rosy. Even after four summits and the inauguration of the secretariat at Kathmandu SAARC could not take up vital areas of co-operation owing to bilateral irritants and strategic discord. Literature on third world regionalism believes that strategic consensus is a basic requirement for the success of regional co-operation in developing areas. In South Asia differences in security perception is a major handicap.

Nonetheless SAARC proved to the world that without common political orientation and threat perception functionally-oriented regional forum could be established without much trouble. Thus SAARC has become an exciting innovation in the realm of regionalism. What is remarkable about this unique model of functional association in a unique region, is the broad consensus existing over a few issues in international political and economic relations, notwithstanding the fact of politico-strategic divergence. Obviously, in the firm footing of non-alignment, harmonised external policy can formally be introduced in the select few areas where similarity of views could be found. What is required is a set of structures and broader range of policies in the functional sphere. However institutional mechanisms resembling the ASEAN structures should not be concocted at this juncture. Prior to the formalisation of external relations informal personal consultations at the higher levels and periodic meetings of officials and ministers of SAARC states required to be encouraged. Mutually agreed upon frequent consultations would pave the way for the development of regional consciousness. Such consultations and exchange of views should stricIty be on informal basis. The relaxed atmosphere inherent in informal contact would help develop personal rapport of the personalities involved in the process of community builidng. In short, Community Formation in SAARC's external relations is an uphill task.

Notes

1. Thomas S. Cox, "Northern Actors in a South-South setting: External Aid and East African Integration", *Journal of Common Market Studies*, Vol. XXI, No. 3, March 1983, p. 283.

2. Willy Brand, *North-South : A Programme for Survival* (London, 1980), p. 18.
3. *Ibid.*
4. Lynn H. Mytelka, "Regulating Direct Foreign Investment and Technology Transfer in the Andean Group," *Journal of Peace Research*, No. 2, Vol. XIV, 1977, p. 156.
5. Lawrence Ziring, "Political Dilemmas and Instability in South and South-West Asia," *Asian Affairs*, Spring, 1983, p. 37.
6. Agha Shahi, "The strategy for peace and security in South Asia," *Strategic Studies*, Vol. VI, Winter/Spring, 1982, No. 2 & 3, p. 16.
7. E. Raymond Plating, "Crisis Pretentious Ideologies and Super Power Behaviour," *Orbis*, Fall, 1981, p. 511.
8. S.D. Muni, "Political Imperatives and the SAARC." Research Paper, p. 2.
9. *Ibid.*
10. S.D. Muni, "Building Regionalism from Below", *Asian Survey*, Vol. XXV, No. 4, April 1985, p. 401.
11. Khadga Bikram Shah & Shridhar Khatri, "The Future of South Asian Regional Co-operation: Some issues in a Nepolise Perspective," *Strategic Studies Series*, No. 3, Spring 1965, p. 32.
12. Department of State Bulletin, Vol. 85, No. 2095, p. 26.
13. *Ibid.*
14. *Indian Express* (Cochin), 7 December 1985; Current Policy, No. 953.
15. *Indian Express* (Delhi), 27 September 1986; United States Department of State, Bureau of Public Affairs, Washington, D.C. Current Policy, No. 953.
16. *POT* (Bangladesh Series), Part 148, 24 July 1980, p. 1329.
17. *Beijing Review*, No. 31, 4 August, 1980.
18. Cited in *Beijing Review*, No. 46, 16 November, 1981.
19. Manoranjan Mohanthy, "China and South Asia", *World Focus*, Vol. 47-48, November-December 1983, p. 69.
20. *Indian Express* (Cochin), 9 December 1985.
21. *Patriot*, 25 November, 1986.
22. *Ibid.*
23. S.D. Muni, "Prospects for SAARC", *Mainstream*, Vol. XXVI, No. 45, 20 August 1988, p. 12.
24. Text of the Delhi Declaration.
25. SAARC Charter.
26. Declaration of ASEAN Concord.
27. R.P. Anand, P.V. Quisumbing, eds., *ASEAN: Identity Development and Culture* (Quezon city, 1981), p. 382.
28. Sheldon W. Siamon, *The ASEAN States and Regional Security* (Stanford, 1982), p. XIII.
29. Quoted in Rogar Irvine, "The Formative Years of ASEAN: 1967-1975," in Alison Bronosvski, ed., *Understanding ASEAN* (London, 1982), p. 14.
30. Astri Suhrke, "Lessons in Regional Co-operation," *Indian Express* (Cochin), 9 November, 1985.

31. K.P. Saksena, *Inter-Government Consultation Systems for Regional Co-operation* (ICWA, New Delhi, 1983), Mimeo, p. 115.
32. Michael Antolik, "ASEAN and SAARC Revisited: More Lessons," *Contemporary South East Asia*, Vol. 9, No. 3, December 1987, p. 221.

CHAPTER VII

CONCLUSION

This study started with a discussion of the important approaches to the concept of regionalism with a view to make use of it for the study of the process of regional co-operation in South Asia. This is followed by a discussion of the major aspects of SAARC regionalism against a comparative perspective and the backdrop of bilateral political issues and external relations in South Asia in order to draw lessons from other regions and associations.

In this chapter the possibilities and limitations of the integration theory are briefly presented.

Classical functionalism as developed by David Mitrany is one of the early theories which considered in a detailed manner the problem of peace and co-operation. It can be stated safely that functionalism is the organisational approach to integration because it envisaged well-knit structures for the purposes of technical self-determination aimed at the ultimate emergence of a community of nations. Functionalism in fact represents a global approach which cuts across the boundaries erected by states and regions. Mitrany wrote that "the regional idea would have vastly different consequences if used to set up closed political units." Thus it is very clear that the functionalist form of regional integration is an approach to international order. Functionalism considered geographic exclusions as an impediment to the growing globalism of technology and welfare. This theory is found infeasible even in post-World War II Europe, because no state was willing to surrender national sovereignty to some supranational authority. While taking the specific case of SAARC, functionalism has got only a very limited relevance.

The association has not yet taken any of the important functional domains for multilateral co-operation. SAARC Audio-visual exchange, food security reserve, sports and games, film festival and some other items touching only the periphery have been discussed. However SAARC has contributed toward a 'Working Peace System' in the sense that peaceful settlement of outstanding disputes are now seriously debated in

South Asia. But SAARC is not at all interested in functional goals of supranationality. SAARC is highly limited in scope and dimension.

Neo-functionalists borrowed heavily from the functionalist school and enriched the theory with the concept of spill-over. The ultimate goal is the supranational handling of economic and political issues to ensure regional peace. Neo-functionalism has been evaluated by eminent scholars and characterised as "Federation by stealth", Crypto-federalism", "Nation-writ large" and "Regional state building". The key concept in the neo-functional theory is the "expansive logic of sector integration" using the mechanism of spill-over, from the technical to the political. The politics of force and coercion had been underplayed by economics. Welfare-oriented supranational structure would be erected using the spill-over process as the mechanism. In the case of SAARC supranational structure limiting the national sovereignty is not at all a desired goal. Thus the spill-over process from technical to the political, is hardly possible. The only possibility is the spill-over in reverse – from the political to the technical. Haas and other neo-functionalists visualised that the future international system would be a network of international organisations and as a result state sovereignty would fade away, slowly, but surely. What Haas and others expected has not come true. State sovereignty and nationalism are still a vibrant force in formulating state behaviour, at least in developing areas. What is available in a third world situation is not supranationalism but inter-governmentalism aimed at the harmonisation of interests in a select few areas. Deutsch argued that the analysis of the transaction flows could help discover and measure regional community. It was criticised that transactions could only describe integration and not cause it. It is well known that the transactional contacts among the members of the SAARC systems are far fewer when compared to the communication and other transactions the SAARC members have with other countries of the world. It is to be mentioned here that direct telephone contacts have been established among the South Asian capitals only after the official launching of SAARC in Dhaka in 1985. Till then telephone contacts between South Asian capitals had been made through Washington, London and Hongkong.

Deutchian concept of security community has been discussed to find out its applicability to the study and analysis of bilateral interaction in South Asia and found interesting. Creation of regional peace is the sole concern of this approach. By using the attributes of the pluralistic security community, analysis of the existing pattern of bilateral relations in South Asia was attempted to realise that it was not easy to apply to

South Asia because the concept has not been developed beyond the mere description of presence or absence of security community. One can easily agree with the criticism levelled against the concept by Nye that it would be very difficult to construct a scale of security community. However this concept is useful in the sense that it contributed to the understanding of regional co-operation and settlement of conflicts. The functional, neo-functional and communication approaches in integration proved infeasible in a third world region like that of South Asia. The supranational handling of political and economic issues are not possible in a developing region, where sovereignty is 'jealously' guarded. This is not to say that the handsome literature on integration theories are totally irrelevant for the study and analysis of regional co-operation in South Asia. An integration scheme established for development should have complex institutions and broader range of policies to deal with the political implications of economic integration. In other words, a relatively high level of political integration is a primary requirement for an integration scheme for collective self-reliance. The third world integration model as provided by Lynn Mytelka is found useful in the South Asian context. Mytelka's Type-III model considers the conditions of dependence and lists measures to reduce dependence. Thus this model is best suited to the conditions of underdevelopment. But it is very difficult to attain Type-III integration scheme in South Asia. Nationalist pulls and pressures, nature of leadership, domestic political conditions and extra-regional factors play a key role in South Asian countries.

Since 'primacy of the political' has been underscored in a third world integration scheme, relatively high degree of political integration at the outset is the logical first step. This high level political integration has got two aspects *viz.*, Bilateral and External. In this the external aspect is considered as the first step towards regional integrative scheme. Primacy should be given to community formation in SAARC's external relations. Projection of common regional front in dealing with external powers will have a spill-over effect on bilateral relations. In other words, collective external relations will help improve bilateral relations in South Asia. Thus external integrative aspect is of primary importance in South Asia.

However without improving bilateral relations, vital economic areas cannot be brought under the regional scheme. At the present stage 'deepening' rather than 'widening' the scope of regionalism should be given priority. The attempts should be to diminish the dimensions of conflict rather than the outright elimination of it. Informal personal consultations at the higher levels and periodic meetings of officials and ministers have had a mollifying effect on strained bilateral relations. The role of the leadership is extremely important. A leadership committed to the cause of multilateral co-operation can induce a sense of accommodation among the people of the participating countries. Periodic visits of leaders and exchanges of views would help improve bilateral relations. SAARC is a compound of interests. Settling of bilateral disputes is not mathematically achievable.

SAARC has not yet obtained group solidarity to deal collectively with the pressures and challenges coming from extra-regional sources. However South Asian leaders are well aware of the importance of developing a regional culture to respond collectively to outside actors, even though there exists disagreement with regard to the approaches to peace and security in South Asia. For instance the Delhi Declaration on South Asian regional co-operation is "mindful of the Declaration on collective self-reliance among non-aligned and other developing countries adopted at the Seventh Non-aligned Summit held at New Delhi which called upon all countries concerned to mobilise all necessary resources and deploy the requisite means in support of sub-regional, regional and inter-regional co-operation among non-aligned and other developing countries." But the Delhi Declaration of August 1983 did not say anything definitely about harmonisation of foreign policies or unified stand in dealing with non-members.

Art. 1 of the SAARC Charter says that the objective of the Association shall be, among other things, "to strengthen co-operation among themselves in internatioanl forums on matters of common interests and to co-operate with international and regional organisations with similar aims and purposes. These objectives of the SAARC would go in conformity with the UN General Assembly Resolution of 16 December 1971, on Indian Ocean. This resolution wanted to exclude great power rivalries and competition as well as bases conceived in the context of such rivalries and competition from the Indian Ocean area.

At this stage a modest attempt can be made to summarise the findings in the present study:

1. Reorientation of foreign policy goals. A shift in emphasis is required in foreign policy goals of the major partners, from that of secuirty to economic development.
2. The arms race betwen India and Pakistan have to be put an end to create an environment of enduring peace in the region.

3. India needs to be patient and sympathetic towards her neighbours.
4. It is the responsibility of India to create an atmosphere of understanding in South Asia because of India's pivotal position.
5. Permanent structures have to be created for regular exchange of views to find solutions to outstanding bilateral political issues.
6. External financial help should be avoided as far as possible.
7. India should adopt a low profile at all times. The initiative to widen the scope of regional co-operation by including core economic areas such as trade, industry, energy, money and finance must come from other partners especially from Pakistan.
8. Efforts should be made to establish a regional mechanism to conduct external relations in those areas that are mutually beneficial.

Efforts in these directions will lay the foundations for a meaningful regional co-operation in the South Asian region.

APPENDICES

Appendix A

SAARC Countries in Comparative Perspective

	Population (million) 1985	Area thousand sq.km.	GNP per capita 1985 (US $)	Average annual growth rate (per cent) GDP 1980-85	GNP 1980-85	Population 1980-85	Average annual rate inflation (per cent) 1980-85
Bangladesh	100.6	144	150	3.6	0.6	2.6	11.5
Bhutan	1.2	47	160	–	–	2.2	–
India	765.1	3,288	270	5.2	1.6	2.2	7.8
Maldives	-	.3	320	–	–	–	–
Nepal	16.5	141	160	3.4	0.2	2.4	8.4
Pakistan	96.2	804	380	6.0	2.5	3.1	8.1
Sri Lanka	15.8	66	380	5.1	2.9	1.4	14.7

Source: World Bank Development Report 1987.

Appendix B

Charter of the South Asian Association for Regional Co-operation

We, the Heads of State or Government of BANGLADESH, BHUTAN, INDIA, MALDIVES, NEPAL, PAKISTAN and SRI LANKA:

1. *Desirous* of promoting peace, stability, amity and progress in the region through strict adherence to the principles of the UNITED CHARTER and NON-ALIGNMENT, particularly respect for the principles of sovereign equality, territorial integrity, national independence, non-use of force and non-interference in the internal affairs of other states and peaceful settlement of all disputes;
2. *Conscious* that in an increasingly interdependent world the objectives of peace, freedom, social justice and economic prosperity are best achieved in the SOUTH ASIAN region by fostering mutual understanding, good neighbourly relations and meaningful co-operation among the Member States which are bound by ties of history and culture;
3. *Aware* of the common problems, interests and aspirations of the peoples of SOUTH ASIA and the need for joint action and enhanced co-operation within their respective political and economic systems and cultural traditions;
4. *Convinced* that regional co-operation among the countries of SOUTH ASIA is mutually beneficial, desirable and necessary for promoting the welfare and improving the quality of life of the peoples of the region;
5. *Convinced* further that economic, social and technical co-operation among the countries of SOUTH ASIA would contribute significantly to national and collective self-reliance;
6. *Recognizing* that increased co-operation, contacts and exchanges among the countries of the region will contribute to the promotion of friendship and understanding among their peoples;

Mishra, A.N., *The Diplomatic Triangle: China-India-America* (Patna, 1980).

Mishra, K.P., Rasgotra, M., Chopra, V.D., eds., *Southern Asia-Pacific: Perceptions and Strategies* (New Delhi, 1988).

Mishra, P.K., *India, Pakistan, Nepal and Bangladesh: India as a factor in the Intra-Regional Integration in South Asia* (Delhi, 1979).

Mishra, Pramod, K., *South Asia in International Politics* (Delhi, 1984).

Mitrany, David, *A Working Peace System* (Chicago: Quardrangle Books, 1966).

Moran, Theodse H., *Multinational Corporation and the Politics of Dependence: Copper in Chile* (Princeton, 1975).

Muni, S.D., and Muni, Anuradha, *Regional Co-operation in South Asia* (New Delhi, 1984).

Nehru, Jawaharlal, *India's Foreign Policy: Selected Speeches,* September 1946-April 1961, (Delhi: Publication Division, Government of India, 1983).

Naidu, M.V.: *Alliances and Balance of Power* (New Delhi, 1974).

Nye, J.S., *Peace in Parts: Integration and Conflict in Regional Organisation* (Boston, 1971).

OECD, *Development Co-operation Efforts and Policies of the Members of the Development Asistance Committee, 1978 Reviews* (Paris, 1978).

Organiski, A., *The Stages of Political Development* (New York, 1965).

Pentland, Charles, *International Theory and European Integration* (London, 1973).

Picus, John, *Trade Aid and Development: The Rich and Poor Nations* (New York, 1967).

Qureshi, M.L., *Survey of Economic Resources and Prospects of South Asia* (Colombo, 1981).

Rhodes, Robert I., ed., *Imperialism and Underdevelopment:* A Reader (New York, 1970).

Richard A. Falk, *The Endangered Planet* (New York, 1971).

Roseanu, James, ed., *Linkage Politics* (New York, 1969).

Rothstein, Robert L., *Global Bargaining, UNCTAD the Quest for a New International Economic Order* (Princeton, 1979).

Saksena, K.P., *Inter-Government Consultation Systems for Regional Co-operation: A Background Study for South Asian Co-operation* (New Delhi: ICWA, 1983).

Satyamurthy, M., ed., *South Asian Regional Co-operation* (Hyderabad, 1982).

Singer, J. David, ed., *Quantitative International Politics: Insights and Evidence* (New York: Free Press, 1968).

Singh, Lalit Prasad, *The Politics of Economic Co-operation in Asia* (Columbia, 1966).

Sukgwal, B.L., *India: A Political Geography* (Bombay, 1971).

Varma, S.P. and Mishra, K.P., ed., *Foreign Policies in South Asia* (Bombay, 1969).

Veiner, Jacob., *The Customs Union Issues* (New York, 1950).

Verner, J., Feld and Gavin Boyd., eds., *Comparative Regional Systems West and East Europe, North America, The Middle East and Developing Countries* (New York, 1980).

Willber, C. ed., *The Political Economy of Development and Under-development* (New York, 1973).

Wionczek, Miguel S., ed., *Latin American Economic Integration Experience and Prospects* (New York, 1966).

Wionczek, Miguel S., *Economic Co-operation in Latin America, Africa and Asia: A Handbook of Documents* (Cambridge, 1969).

Wolpert, Stanley. *Roots of Conformation in South Asia* (New York: Oxford University Press, 1982).

Yu, George T., ed., *Intra-Asian International Relations* (Boulder, 1977).

Secondary Sources: Articles

A.A.D.S.D., "International seminar on regional co-operation as a means of realising collective self-reliance" Congo-Brazaville, 16-18 May, 1983, *development and Socio-economic progress* (1) January March 1984, pp. 3-156. (Series of articles)

Abeyesekara, Charles, "Issues of South Asian Co-operation : A Sri Lankan perspective", *Strategic studies series*, No. 1, Spring 1985, pp. 152-62.

Abraham, A.S., "Co-operation in South Asia: Seven States in Search of a Link", *Times of India* (New Delhi) 24, March '81.

Adiseshiah, Malcom S., "Economic Rationale of SAARC", *South Asia Journal*, Vol. I, No. 1, July-September, pp. 29-42.

Aditya Anand, SAARC: "The Call for Co-operation and Concept of a South Asian Regime", *South Asia Forum*, No. 7, 1984.

Agarwal, A.K., "Eighth Finance Commission Report: A Critique", *Southern Economist*, Vol. 23, No. 12, October 15, 1984, pp. 17-18.

Agarwal, Govid Ram, "Some Avenues for South Asian Economic Co-operation", *South Asia Journal*, Vol. I, No. 1, July-September 1987.

Agarwal, Mangat Ram "Regional Economic Co-operation : A Strategy for Economic Development in the South and South-East Asian Region", *Asian profile*, Vol. 12, December, 1984, pp. 537-54.

Ahamad Bashir., "Sharing of River Waters in South Asia". *Regional Studies,* Vol. 3., No. 2, September 1985, pp. 16-20.

----, "SAARC: Some Reflections", *Regional Studies,* Vol. 5, No. 4, Autumn 1987, pp. 3-6.

Ahmar, Moonis, "Politics of Conflict and Co-operation in South Asia", *Pakistan Horizon*, Vol. 35, No. 3, 1982.

Ahmed, Emajuddin, "Regional Co-operation in South Asia and India's role", *IDSA Journel,* Vol. 15, No. 3, January-March 1983, pp. 405-22.

Ahmed, Iftikhar, "Technology, Production Linkages and Women's Employment in South Asia", *International Labour Review*, Vol. 126, No. 1, January-February, 1987, pp. 21-40.

Ahmed, Masood, "Capital, Labour and Output Trends in Pakistan, 1969-70 to 1979-80" *Pakistan Economic and Social Review*, Vol. 20, No. 2, Winter 1982, pp. 1982-91.

Ahmed, Samina, "South Asian Regional Co-operation", *Regional Studies,* Vol. I, No. 3, Summer 1983.

----, "Pakistan's Proposal for a Nuclear Weapon Free Zone in South Asia", *Pakistan Horizon*, Fourth Quarter, 1979.

Ahmed, Sultan, "Filling the Void in South Asia", *Indian and Foreign Review*, Vol. 20, No. 20 August, 1-4, 1983.

Ahuja, Kanta, "Trends in Regional Economic Co-operation in South and South East Asia". *South Asian Studies*, Vol. 12, Nos. 1-2, January-December 1977.

Akbar, M.J., *Sunday* (Calcutta), 19 June 1982.

Akram, A.I. "Policy and Postures in South Asia", *Regional Studies,* Vol. 5, No. 2, Spring 1987, pp. 3-25.

Aksan, Abul, "New Horizons for SAARC", *Mainstream*, Vol. 25, Annual Special, 1987, p. 57.

Al-Gumer, Jassion, "Co-operation in Hydrocarbons", *Pakistan and Gulf Economist*, Vol. 6, No. 21. May 1987, pp. 20-1.

Ali, Ifzal, ''Estimating the Determinants of Export Supply in India'', *Indian Economic Journal*, Vol. 31, No. 3, January-March 1984, pp. 13-23.

Ali, Salamat, ''An ill-wind in the East'', *Far Eastern Economic Review* Vol. 130, No. 50, December 19, 1985, pp. 26-28.

Antolik, Michael, ''ASEAN and SAARC Revisited: More Lessons'', *Contemporary South East Asia*, Vol. 9, No.3, December 1987, pp. 221-28.

Armacost, Michael, ''South Asia and U.S. Foreign Policy'', *Department of State Bulletin*, Vol. 2, No. 2, June-August 1984, pp. 177-99.

Attiga, Ali Ahmed, ''South-South Co-operation is Essential'', *Pakistan and Gulf Economist*, Vol. 6, No. 17, April 25, 1987, pp. 40-2.

Axline, W. Andrew, ''Underdevelopment, Dependency and Integration: The Politics of Regionalism in the Third World'', *International Organisation*, Vol. XXXI, No. 1, Winter 1977, pp. 82-106.

Bagchi, S.K., ''Trade Development in South Asia'', *Foreign Trade Review*, Vol. 10, No. 1, April-June 1975.

Baker, Christopher, ''Economic Re-organisation and the slump in South East Asia'', *Comparative Studies in Soviet and History*, July-1981.

Balihatlhet, Kenneth, ''Rewriting of South Asian History by South Asian Historians after 1947'', *Asian Affairs*, Vol. 15, No. February, 1984, pp. 27-38.

Baliga, B.R., ''World Views and Multinational Corporations Investments in the Less Developed Economies''. *Columbia, Journal of World Business*, Vol. 19, No. 2, Summer 1984, pp. 80-84.

Banerjee, Subrata, ''SAARC, Problems and prospect, *PTI Feature*, Vol. 6, No. 174, December 2, 1985, PF - B 720.

Banerjee, Summanta, ''India and South Asia: Growing Economic Stake'', *Economic and Political Weekly*, 12 June 1971.

Banskota, N.P., ''Nepal: Toward Regional Economic Co-operation in South Asia'', *Asian Survey*, Vol. 21, No. 3, March 1981.

Baral, Lok Raj, ''Nepal's Security Policy and South Asian Regionalism'', *Asian Survey*, Vol. 26, No., 11 November 1986, pp. 1207-19.

Berindranath, Dewan, ''South Asia Co-operation : A Case of Caution'', *Democratic World*, Vol. 10, No. 18, May 3, 1981.

Bhandari, Ramesh: ''South Asia Summit'', *Mainstream*, Vol. XXIV, No. 13 & 14, 30 November 1985.

Bhatia, B.M., ''Food Security in South Asia''. *India Quarterly*, Vol. 40. Nos 3 & 4, July-December 1984, pp. 301-13.

Bhatt, P.R. ''Trade Flows in South Asia'', *Man & Development*, Vol. 6, No. 3, September 1984, pp. 104-16.

Bhatnagar, Nandita, ''Development of Water Resources in South Asia'', *Biss Journal* , Vol. 6, No. 3, July 1985, pp. 287-313.

Bhaumik, Kirit, ''Dacca's Initiative: Idealism and Pragmatism'', *World Focus*, Vol. 3, No. 3, March 1982.

Boomely, Danial, W., and Chapagain, Deudrap, ''Village Against the Centre: Resource Depletion in South Asia'', *American Journal of Agricultural Economics*, Vol. 66, No. 5, December 1984, pp. 868-73.

Boris, Dieter, ''Problems of Regional Economic Integration in the Third World Exemplified by The Central American Common Market (MCCA) and the Andean Pact'', *Development & Socio-Economic Progress*, No. 2, January-March 1984, pp. 116-32.

Bhambhri, C.P. ''International Capitalism and Indian Erosion of National Independence'', *Asian Affairs,* Vol. 5, No. 1, January-March 1983, pp. 1-16.

Brams, Steven, ''Transaction Flows in the International System'', *The American Political Science Review,* Vol. LX, No. 4, December 1966, pp. 880-98.

Brajovic, Rade, ''In South Asia: The Big and the Small''. *Review of International Affairs*, Vol. 33, No. 763, January, 20.

Braun, Dieter, Change in South Asia Intraregional and External Relationships'', *World Today*, Vol. 34, No. 10, October 1978.

Braun, Dieter, ''South Asia and the Arc of Crisis: Interaction of Regional and External Policies'', 1971-82, *Problems of Non-alignment*, Vol. I, No. 13, September-November 1983, pp. 215-26.

Brenner, Michael, ''Strategic Consequences of Nuclear Proliferation in South Asia for Iran'', *Journal of Strategic Studies*, Vol. 8, No. 4, December 185, pp. 59-66.

Brij, Mohan, ''Trade Prospects: India's Leading Role''. *World Focus*, Vol. 3, No. 3, March 1982.

Cantori, Louis J. and Steven L., Spiegel, ''The Analysis of Regional International Politics: The Integration *versus* the Empirical Systems Approach'', *International Organisation* , Vol. XXVII, No. 4, Autumn 1973, pp. 465-94.

Caparaso, James A., ''Theory and Method in the Study of International Integration'', *International Organisation*, Vol. XXV, No. 2, Spring 1971, pp. 228-253.

Caparaso, James A., "The External Consequence of Regional Integration for Pan-European Relations", *International Studies Quarterly*, Vol. XX, No. 3, September 1976, pp. 341-392.

Chadwick, R.W. and Karl Deutsch, "International Trade and Economic Integration: Further Developments in Trade Matrix Analysis". *Comparative Political Studies,* Vol. 6, No. 1, April 1973, pp. 84-109.

Chakravarthy, Nikhil, "South Asia as a Concept", *World Focus*, Vol. 6, No. 9, September 1985, pp. 15-18.

——, "Concept of South Asia", *Mainstream*, Vol. 25, February 18, 1984, pp. 10-12.

Chakravarthy, Sumit, "SAARC Survives Subversion", *Mainstream*, Vol. 25, No. 41, June 27, 1987, pp. 4-5, 34.

Chanana, Charanjit, "South Asian Economic Community", *Asian Economist*, Vol. 4, February, 1978.

——, "South Asia: The Changing Environment", *South Asian Studies*, Vol. 16, No. 1, January-June 1981.

Chicherov, Alexander, "South Asia and the Indian Ocean in the 1980's: Some Trends Towards Changes in International Relations", *Asian Survey*, Vol. 24, No. 11, November 1984, pp. 1117-30.

Cohen, Stephen, "South Asia After Afghanistan", *Problems of Communism* Vol. 34, No. 1, January-February 1985, pp. 18-31.

Chopra, Pran, "Regional Co-operation," *World Focus*, Vol. 4, Nos, 11-12, November-December, 1983.

——, "The Search for South Asia," *Perspective,* Vol. 1, No. 8, March, 1978.

——, "Why South Asia and How," *Word Focus*, Vol. 3, No. 3, March 1982.

——, "Facts and Fiction of Inequality" *Mainstream* (New Delhi), Vol. XXIV, No. 13 & 14, November 1985.

Colonialism, *South Asia Bulletin*, Spring 1985, pp. 1-45 (Series of Articles).

"Slow Steps Towards South Asian Co-operation", *Commerce*, Vol. 149, No. 3821, August 25, 1984, pp. 305-8.

"New Era in South Asian Regional Co-operation", *Commerce*, Vol. 151, No. 3891, December 21, 1985, pp. 1097-1102.

Corea Gamani, "Regional Co-operation in South Asia: Perspective and Prospects", *South Asia Journal*, Vol. 1, No. 1, July-September 1987, pp. 1-6.

7. *Recalling* the DECLARATION signed by their Foreign Ministers in NEW DELHI on August 2, 1983 and *noting* the progress achieved in regional co-operation;

8. *Reaffirming* their determination to promote such co-operation within an institutional framework;

DO HEREBY AGREE to establish an organisation to be known as SOUTH ASIAN ASSOCIATION FOR REGIONAL CO-OPERATION, hereinafter referred to as the ASSOCIATION, with the following objectives, principles, institutional and financial arrangements:

Article I

Objectives

The objectives of the ASSOCIATION shall be:

a. to promote the welfare of the peoples of SOUTH ASIA and to improve their quality of life;

b. to accelerate economic growth, social progress and cultural development in the region and to provide all individuals the opportunity to live in dignity and to realize their full potentials;

c. to promote and strengthen collective self-reliance among the countries of SOUTH ASIA;

d. to contribute to mutual trust, understanding and appreciation on one another's problems;

e. to promote active collaboration and mutual assistance in the economic, social, cultural, technical and scientific fields;

f. to strengthen co-operation with other developing countries;

g. to strengthen co-operation among themselves in international forums on matters of common interests ; and

h. to co-operate with international and regional organisations with similar aims and purpose.

Article II

Principles

1. Co-operation within the framework of the ASSOCIATION shall be based on respect for the principles of sovereign equality, territorial integrity, political independence, non-interference in the internal affairs of other States and mutual benefit.

2. Such co-operation shall not be a substitute for bilateral and multilateral co-operation but shall complement.

3. Such co-operation shall not be inconsistent with bilateral and multilateral obligation.

Article III

Meeting of the Heads of State or Government

The Heads of State or Government shall meet once a year or more often as and when considered necessary by the Member States.

Article IV

Council of Ministers

1. A Council of Ministers consisting of the Foreign Ministers of the Member States shall be established with the following functions:

   a. formulation of the policies of the ASSOCIATION;
   b. review of the progress of co-operation under the ASSOCIATION;
   c. decision on new areas of co-operation;
   d. establishment of additional mechanism under the ASSOCIATION as deemed necessary;
   e. decision on other matters of general interest of the ASSOCIATION.

The Council of Ministers shall meet twice a year. Extraordinary session of the Council may be held by agreement among the Member States.

Article V

Standing Committee

1. The Standing Committee comprising the Foreign Secretaries shall have the following functions:

   a. overall monitoring and co-ordination of programme of co-operation;
   b. approval of projects and programmes, and the modalities of their financing;
   c. determining of inter-sectoral priorities;

Commerce. ''Trade A South Asian Economic Community'', *Commerce*, Vol. 146, No. 3752, April 30, 1983 (Editorial).

Correspondent, Pseud, ''SARC: Road to Summit'', *Mainstream*, Vol. 47, July 21, 1984.

——, ''SARC: Intentions and Implementation'', *Mainstream*, Vol. 22, No. 27, March 3, 1984.

Commerce, ''South Asian Regional Co-operation'', *Commerce*, Vol. 147, No. 3768, August 20 (Editorial).

Cranstion, Alan, ''Nuclear Proliferation and US National Security Interests,'' *Strategic Digest*, Vol. 14, No. 8, August 1984, pp. 825-33.

Current History, The Nations of South Asia, *Current History*, Vol. 81, No. 475, May 1982, pp. 193-234.

Damodaran, A.K. 'South Asia and U.S.'', *Mainstream*, Vol. 23, No. 6, October 6, 1984, pp. 15-8, 34.

Dasgupta, Punya Priya, ''SAARC Session – till we meet again'', *Herald Review*, Vol. 1, No. 32, May 27-June 2, 1985, pp. 32-34.

Dasgupta, Subhendu, ''Political Economy of SAARC'', *Frontier*, Vol. 19, No. 47, July 11, 1987, pp. 6-9.

Desai, M.V. ''South Asia: Worthwhile Initiatives, *Commerce*, Vol. 148, No. 3798, March 19, 1984.

Desai, Ashok, V., ''New Forms of International investment in India'', *Social Scientist*, Vol. 12, No. 6, January 1984, pp. 23-45.

Desai, M.V. ''Area Studies in Regional Co-operation: State Aid Marred by Official Indifference?, *Mainstream*, Vol. 22, Nos. 3-7, Annual No. 1983.

De Silva, Dfatton, ''Tacking Environmental Problems'', *Commerce*, Vol. 142, No. 3641, March 28, 1981, pp. 673-4.

Dilara Choudhury, ''Major Powers Involvement in South Asia'', *Biss Journal*, Vol. 7, No. 3, 1986, pp. 307-341.

D.N. Pseud, India's Role in South Asia, *Economic and Political Weekly*, Vol. 23, No. 30, July 23, 1988, pp. 1512-3.

Engineer, Asghar, Ali, ''Ethnic Conflict in South Asia'', *Economic and Political Weekly*, Vol. 22, No. 13, March 28, 1987, pp. 540-2.

Farmer, B.H., ''Perspectives on the Green Revolution in South Asia'', *Modern Asian Studies*, Vol. 20, No. 1, February 1986, pp. 75-200.

Fifield, Russell, H., ''South-East Asia as a Regional Concept'', *South Asian Journal of Social Science*, Vol. II, No. 2, 1983, pp. 1-14.

Galtung John, "A Structural Theory of Imperialism", *Journal of Peace Research*, 2(1971), pp. 82-117.

----, "A Structural Theory of Integration", *Journal of Peace Research*, 4(1968), pp. 375-95.

Gandhi, Indira, "Inaugural address at the South Asian Regional Co-operation meeting of Foreign Ministers at New Delhi", August 1, 1983, *India* Quarterly, Vol. 40, Nos. 3 & 4, July-December 1984, pp. 259-61.

Gangal S.C., "Spotlight on South Asia: Co-operation and Crisis in the Region", *Gandhi Marg*, Vol. 5, No. 6, September 1983, pp. 311-14.

Gapar, John, "IMF Policies and the Developing Countries: A Third World Perspective", *Indian Journal of Economics*, Vol. 64, No. 24, April 1984, pp. 437-48.

Gelb, Leslie, H., "Pakistan's Link Perils U.S.-China Nuclear Pact", *Strategic Digest*, Vol. 14, No. 13, August 1984, pp. 834-36.

Ghosh, Chitra, "Rural Backwardness and Strategies of Development in the Third World", *Asian Studies*, Vol. 5, No. 2, April-June 1987, pp. 18-29.

Gosh, Partha S., "Terrorism and SAARC", *India Quarterly*, Vol. 43, No. 2, April-June 1987, pp. 121-37.

Ghosh, Partha, S., "Ethnic and Religious Conflicts in South Asia", *Conflict Studies*, No. 178, pp. 1-19.

Gonsalves Eric, "Agenda for the Next Decade", *South Asia Journal*, Vol. I, No.1, July-September, pp. 19-28.

G.P.D., Pseud, "Long Shadow over South Asia, *Economic and Political Weekly*, Vol. 16, No. 47, November 21, 1981.

Gronin, Richard, "Prospects for Nuclear Proliferation in South Asia: *Middle East Journal*, Vol. 37, No. 4, Autumn 1983, pp. 594-616.

Gudha, Amalendu, "How a Self-reliant Development Model for Bangladesh", *Asian Profile*, Vol. 12, No. 1, February 1984, pp. 29-52.

Gudha, Amalendu, "Issue and Strategies of Self-reliance in South Asia", *Asian Profile*, Vol. 9, No. 2, April, 1981.

Gupta, Amita, "Cultural Exchanges in South Asia", *Mainstream*, Vol. XXIV, No. 13-14, 30 November, 1985.

Hass Ernst B., "The Study of Regional Integration: Reflections of the Joy and Anguish of Pre-theorising", *International Organisation*, Vol. XIV, No. 4, Autumn 1970, pp. 705-737.

Has, Ernst B., "The Uniting of Europe and the Uniting of Latin America", *Journal of Common Market Studies,* 5 June 1967, pp. 315-343.

Haas, Richard N, "South Asia: Too Late to Remove the Bomb? *Orbis,* Vol. 32, No. 1, Winter 1988, pp. 107-18.

Hafiz, M. Abdul, "Regional Problems and Prospects for Co-operation in South Asia", *Biss Journal,* Vol. 8, No. 4, October 1987, pp. 385-406.

Haksar, P.N. "Stability and Regional Co-operation", *Mainstream,* Vol. XXIV, No. 13 & 14, 30 November, 1985.

Hansan, Roger D., "Regional Integration: Reflections on a Decade of Theoretical Efforts", *World Politics,* Vol. 21, January 1969, pp. 242-271.

Hardgrave, Robert L., "Why India Matters: The Challenge to American Policy in South Asia", *Asian Affairs,* Vol. II, No. 1, Spring 1984, pp. 45-56.

Harrison, Selig., "American Policy in South Asia: India, Pakistan and on Afghan Settlement", *Mainstream,* Vol. 25, No. 31, April 18, 1987, pp. 7-10.

Hassan, N. Gardezi, "India Revisited", *Mainstream,* 13 December, 1986, Vol. XXV, No. 13.

Honavar, R.M., "South Asian Economics", *IASSI Quarterly Newsletter,* Vol. 3, Nos.1/2, June 1984.

Horn, Robert, C., "Soviet Union and Sino-Indian Relations", *Orbis,* Vol. 26, No. 4, August 1984, pp. 145-56.

Huq, Shamsul, M., "South Asian for Regional Co-operation: Past, Present and Future", *Biss Journal,* Vol. 7, No. 3, 1986, pp. 426-441.

Huq, Shamsul, "Beyond Bangalore", *South Asia Journal,* Vol. 1, No. 1, July-September 1987, pp. 7-18.

Humayun, Kabir Mohammad, "India, SAARC and South Asia", *Regional Studies,* Vol. 4, No. 3, summer 1986, pp. 67-80.

Hussain, T. Karki, "China's Calculus in South Asia" *Mainstream,* Vol. 25, No. May 16, 1987, pp. 11-14.

Iftekharuzzaman, "United States-Bangladesh Relations", *Asian Affairs,* Vol. 5, No. 4, October-December 1983, pp. 399-419.

——, "Regional Co-operation in South Asia: Socio-cultural Imperatives", *Asian Affairs,* Vol. 9, No. 2, April-June 1987, pp. 63-70.

Iftekharuzzaman, "SAARC in Progress: Achievements, Old Problems, New Dimensions", *Regional Studies*, Vol. 6, No. 1, Winter 1987-88 pp. 12-26.

India and Foreign Review "Strengthening Regional Co-operation: SAARC Standing Committee Meets", *Indian & Foreign Review*, Vol. 21, No. 11, March 31, 1984, pp. 8-9, 11.

"India and its Neighbours", *World Focus*, Vol. 6, Nos. 11-12, November-December 1985, pp. 3-79.

"Introducing Maldives", *Indian and Foreign Review*, Vol. 20, No. 20, August 1-14, 1983.

Iqbal, Mohammad, "SAARC: The urge for Co-operation in South Asia", *Regional Studies*, Vol. 4, Autumn, 1986, pp. 47-64.

Islam, Md., Meinul, "Industrial Relations in Bangladesh: Case of a Post-colonial Society Ruled by a Compradore Bourgeoisie", *Asian Affairs*, Vol. 5, No. 1, January-March 1983, pp. 67-68.

Indian Subcontinent, *World Review*, Vol. 24, No. 4, October 1983, pp. 5-10.

International Organisation, Vol. XXIV, No. 4, Autumn 1970.

Jaber, Tayseer, "The Relevance of Traditional Integration Theory to Less Developed Countries, "*Journal of Common Market Studies*, Vol. IX (1971), pp. 254-67.

Jagjit, Singh, "Transport Linkages in South Asia", *India Quarterly*, Vol. 40, Nos. 3, 4, July-December 1984, pp. 277-86.

Jambholkar, V.K.H., "Major Development in India's Foreign Policy and Relations", July-December 1980, *International Studies*, October-December 1982, pp. 445-64.

Jayaramu, P.S., "Politics of Peace Initiatives in the Indian Sub-continent", *Problems of Non-alignment*, Vol. 1, No. 4, December 1983/February 1984, pp. 379-96.

Jayaraman, T.K., "Economic Integration in the Indian Sub-continent", *Asiaweek*, Vol. 6, No. 2, December 1976.

Jazic, Zivojin, "SAARC Summit in Nepal", *Review of International Affairs*, Vol. 39, No. 907, January 20, 1988, pp. 24-26.

Jha, Braj Kishore, "Concept of Political Modernization with particular reference to South Asia", *Teaching Politics,* Vol. 11, No. 1985, pp. 35-49.

Joeck, Neil, "Strategic Consequences of Nuclear Proliferation in South Asia: Introduction", *Journal of Strategic Studies*, Vol. 8, No. 4, December 1985, pp. 3-6.

Jones, Rodiey W., ''Strategic Consequences of Nuclear Proliferation in South Asia: Outlook from the U.S.'' *Journal of Strategic Studies*, Vol. 13, No. 4, December 1985, pp. 28-39.

Joshi, Navin Chandra, ''Need for South Asian Regional Co-operation'', *News from the Non-aligned World*, Vol. 6, No. 2, January 1985, pp. 43-48.

——, ''Asian Regional Economic Co-operation'', *PTI Feature*, Vol. 5, No. 12, October 15, 1984, PF-B 76.

Journal of Strategic Studies', ''Strategic Consequences of Nuclear Proliferation in South Asia'', *Journal of Strategic Studies*, Vol. 8, No. 4, December 1985, pp. 3-109.

Kackar, Rannjana, ''Good Neighbours: An Indepth Report on SAARC'', *Gentleman,* December 1985, pp. 62-76.

Kadeer Ahmed, ''A Concept of Non-alignment and its Impact on South Asia'', *Pakistan Horizon*, Vol. 34, No. 3, 1981.

Kalirajam, K., ''South Co-operation, Trade Relations between Indonesia and South Asia'', *Pakistan Development Review,* Vol. 22, No. 4, Winter 1983, pp. 261-82.

Kansakar, Vidya Bir Singh, ''The Demographic Dimension of Regional Co-operation in South Asia'', *Regional Studies*, No. 3, Spring 1988, pp. 78-79.

Kapur, Pratap, ''SAARC: Whither Regional Co-operation?'' *Democratic World*, Vol. 12, No. 35, August 28, 1983.

Katyal K.K., ''South Asian Summitry so near, yet so far'', *Frontline*, Vol. 2, No. 25, December 14-27, 1985, pp. 4-12.

——, ''SAARC: A Long Trek'', *Frontline*, Vol. 3, No. 22, November 1-14, 1986, pp. 4-9.

——, ''SAARC: Some Lessons, *Frontline* Vol. 4, No. 13, Jun 27, July 10, 1987, pp. 118-20.

Kennedy, Charles, H., Politics of Ethnic Preference in Pakistan'', *Asian Survey*, Vol. 24, No. 6, June 1984, pp. 688-703.

Khalid, Mohammad, ''Regional Solution to Individual Problems'' *Pakistan and Gulf Economist*, Vol. 2, No. 11, March 12, 1983.

Khalilzad, Zalmay, ''Politics of Ethnicity in South-West Asia'' Political Development Political Decay?'' *Political Science Quarterly*, Vol. No. 4, Winter 1984-85, pp. 657-80.

Khan, Ahsan Ali, ''Tamil Question in Historical Perspective: Its Impact on Indo-Sri Lankan Relations'', *Pakistan Horizon*, Vol. 37, No. 2, 1984, pp. 42-71.

Khan, Ahsan Ali, "Military Balance in South Asia", *Asia Pacific Community*, No. 25, Summer 1984, pp. 100-116.

Khan, Naheed Murtza, "India, South Asian Regional Co-operation and Detente", *Detente*, Vol. 4, No. 1, October-November, 1984.

Khan, Nixon, Athony Aitmad, "South Asia Detente and Co-operation or Confrontation", *Foreign Affairs Report*, Vol. 31, No. 7, July 1982.

Khan, Rashid Ahmad, , "China's Policy Toward South Asia: A Comparative Perspective", *Regional Studies*, Vol. 5, No. 1, Winter 1986/87, pp. 14-27.

-----, *Pakistan Horizon*, Vol. 37, No. 3, 1984, pp. 37-48.

Khan, Resheeduddin, "Problems of Nation Building", *World Focus*, Vol. 4, Nos. 11-12, November-December 1983.

Khan, Zillur Rahman, "Role of Ideology and Leadership in South Asian Co-operation Movement", *Asian Affairs*, Vol. 9, No. 2, April-June 1987, pp. 1-17.

Khilhani, N.M., "SAARC: An Ideal South Asian Forum", *PTI Feature*, Vol. 7, No. 11, October 15, 1986, FC. 213.

Kapur Ashok, "Nuclear Proliferation in South Asian Perspectives", *Pacific Affairs*, Vol. 57, No.2, Summer 1984, pp. 304-10.

Khanna, Ashok, "Market Distortions and Export Performance: India's Exports of Manufacturers in the 1970s", *Review of World Economics*, Vol. 120, No. 2, 1984, pp. 348-60.

Kohli, Atul, "Regime Types and Poverty Reform in India" *Pacific Affairs*, Vol. 56, No. 4, Winter 1983-84, pp. 649-72.

Krislov, Joseph, and Stoup, Robert, H., "What Account for the Varying Growth Rates in India, Pakistan and Bangladesh 1950-1980?", *Asian Profile*, Vol. 13, No. 3, June 1985.

Kumar, Satish, "Regional Co-operation", *Hindustan Times* (New Delhi), 10 September, 1981.

Liljunen, Kimmo, "Trans-national Corporations and Third World Industrialisation", *Conflict and Co-operation*, Vol. 19, No.1, 1984, pp. 39-58.

Majeed, Akhtar, "Indian Defence Policy in South Asia", *Indian Journal of Politics*, Vol. 19, No. 2, June 1984, pp. 75-82.

Malhotra, Inder, "India and its Neighbours", *World Focus*, Vol. 2, Nos. 7-8, July-August 1987, pp. 37-9, 47.

Malla, Gehendra L., "Regional Co-operation in South Asia: A Nepalese Perspective", *Strategic Studies Series*, Nos. 6-7, Winter-Spring 1985-86, pp. 94-120.

Mangat Ram, "Regional Plan Harmonisation and Trade Co-operation in South Asia", *Foreign Trade Review*, Vol. 8, No. 2, July-September 1973.

Mani, Late, and Frankenberg, Ruth, "Challenge of `Oriéntalism", *Economy and Society*, Vol. 14, No. 2, May 1985, pp. 174-92.

Mansergh, Nicholas, "India and Pakistan: Whether they have turned?", *International Journal*, Vol. 34, No. 2, Spring 1984, pp. 460-80.

Mansingh, Surjit, "Regional Co-operation in South Asia: Imperatives and Obstacles", *Punjab Journal of Politics*, Vol. 6, No. 1, January-June 1982, pp. 130-144.

Mass, Citha, D., "Conceptual Analysis of South Asian Regional Co-operation", *IDSA Journal*, Vol. 17, No. 3, January-March, 1985, pp. 272-96.

Mathur, Girish, "SAARC: A still born child", *Link*, Vol. 29, No. 15, November 16, 1986, pp. 6-9.

Matters, A., "Protectionism inside the European Court", *Journal of World Trade Law*, Vol. 18, No. 4, July-August 1984, pp. 283-308.

Menon, M.P.M., "Evaluation of South Asian Regional Co-operation", *Indian and Foreign Review*, Vol. 23, No. 5, December 31, 1985, pp. 4-5.

Mishra, Promod Kumar, "Politics of South Asian Co-operation: A Study in Objective and Viability." *Problems of Non-alignment*, Vol. No. 4, December 1983 – February 1984, pp. 397-436.

——, "South Asia's Quest for an Identity and SAARC", *India Quarterly*, Vol. 40, Nos. 3 & 4, July-December 1984, pp. 314-22.

——, "China and South Asia" *China Report* (New Delhi), Vol. XXI, No. 5, 1985, pp. 403-413.

——, "Bangalore Summit: Bilateralism *versus* Regionalism" *PTI Feature*, Vol. 7, No. 17, November 27, 1986.

——, "Kathmandu: Summit and After", *PTI Feature*, Vol. 8, No. 16, November 16, 1987, PF-C 863.

Mukerjee, I.N., "The Asian Clearing Union: A Step Towards Regional Economic Co-operation in South Asia". *Indian Journal of Asian Studies*, Vol. 1, No. 1, January-June 1977, pp. 20-36.

Mukhopadhyay, Deepankar, "Summit of Hope', *Indian and Foreign Review*, December 31, 1985, pp. 7-11.

Mummen, Thumpy, "Trade Gap Model and IMF Loan to India", *Indian Economic Journal*, Vol. 31, No. 3, January-March 1984, pp. 45-52.

Muni, S.D., "India and Regionalism in South Asia: A Political Perspective", *International Studies*, Vol. 17, Nos. 3-4, July-December 1978, pp. 483-501.

-----, "Reagan's South Asia Policy: The Strategic Dimension", *IDSA Journal*, Vol. 16, No.2, October-December 1983, pp. 132-48.

-----, "NAM and South Asia", *Third World*, 11 January-February 1984, pp. 12-15.

-----, "SARC: The Villingili Ministerial Meeting", *Asian Affairs*, Vol. 6, No.1, January-March 1984, pp. 76-86.

-----, "Systematic and Strategic Divergences: Implications for India's Security", *Mainstream* Vol. XXII, No. 29, March 1984, pp.4-5.

-----, "South Asia: Systematic and Strategic Divergences-II", *Mainstream*, Vol. 22, No. 30, March 24, 1984, pp. 19-22.

-----, "Sri Lanka the August Outrage", *Strategic Analysis*, Vol. 8, No. 6, September 1984, pp. 500-10.

-----, "General's Foray into South Asian Security", *Strategic Analysis*, Vol. 8, No. 7, October 1984, pp. 593-606.

-----, "Sri Lanka's Ethnic Convulsions", *Mainstream*, Vol. 22, Annual 1984, pp. 51-56.

-----, "Political Issues and South Asian Co-operation", *Mainstream* Vol. 24, Nos. 13-14, November 30, 1985, pp. 27-29, 33.

-----, "Focus – South Asian Summit: Primacy of Politics", *Mainstream*, Vol. 24, No. 15, December 14, 1985, pp. 3-4, 6.

-----, "SAARC: Gains of the Leaders, *Mainstream*, Vol. XXIV, No. 16, 21 December, 1985.

-----, "South Asian Regional Co-operation: Evolution and Prospects", *IDSA Journal*, Vol. 19, No.1, July-September 1986, pp. 121-39.

-----, "SAARC and Security, *Mainstream*, Vol. 25, No. 9, November 15, 1986, pp. 30-34.

-----, "SAARC Summit Perspectives", *Mainstream*, Vol. 26, No. 4, November 7, 1987, pp. 5-6.

-----, "Prospects for SAARC", *Mainstream*, Vol. XXVI, No. 45, 20 August 1988, pp. 7-13.

Mytelka, Lynn Krieger, "The Salience of Gains in Third World Integration System", *World Politics*, Vol. XXV, No. 2, January 1973, pp. 236-250.

Mytelka, Lynn K., "Regulation of Direct Foreign Investment and Technology Transfer in the Andean Group", *Journal of Peace Research*, Vol. XIV, no. 2(1977), pp. 155-84.

Naqvi, Syed Navab Haider and Others, "Possibilities of Regional Trade Expansion: A Link Model for Pakistan, India, Bangladesh and Srilanka", *Pakistan Development Review*, Vol. 23, No. 1, Spring 1984, pp. 9-36.

Narasimha Rao, P.V., "Foundation of India's Foreign Policy," *Indian and Foreign Review*, Vol. 19, No. 5, December 15-31, 1981, pp. 8-10.

Nepal, J.B. "Bhutan and SAARC", *Indian and Foreign Review*, Vol. 20, No. 20, August 1-14, 1983, pp. 10-11.

Nizami, Arif, "South Asian Co-operation", *Seminar*, No. 303, November 1984, pp. 34-5.

Noorani, A.G. "Search for New Relationships in the Indian Subcontinent", *World Today*, Vol. 31, No. 6, June 1975, pp. 240-8.

——, "Indo-Pak Treaty" *Indian Express* (Cochin), 10 January 1986.

Nihal Singh, S., "Why India Goes to Moscow for Arms", *Asian Survey*, Vol. 24, No. 7, July 1984, pp. 707-20.

Nye Joseph S., "Patterns and Catalysts in Regional Integration", *International Organisation*, Vol. XIX, No. 4, Autumn 1965, pp. 870-884.

Nye, Joseph, S., "Comparative Regional Integration Concept and Measurement", *International Organisation*, Vol. XXII, No. 4, Autumn 1968, pp. 855-80.

Nye, Joseph and Robert Keochane, Transnational Relations and World Politics: An Introduction", *International Organisation*, Vol. XXV, No. 3, Summer 1971, pp. 329-50.

Nye, Joseph S., "Comparing Common Markets: A Revised Neofunctionalist Model", *International Organisation*, Vol. XXIV, No. 50, Autumn 1970, pp. 796-35.

'Pakistan and Gulf Economist', "Regional Co-operation of South Asian Countries", *Pakistan and Gulf Economist*, Vol. 2, No. 31, July 30, 1983, pp. 5-6.

----- , "The South Asian Basket", *Pakistan and Gulf Economist*, Vol. 11, No. 15, April 9, 1983, pp. 6-7.

——, "South Asia's Group of 7" *Pakistan and Gulf Economist*, Vol. 3, No. 39, September 29, 1984, pp. 6-7.

Panda, Rajaram, "Regionalism as an Approach to Peace: A Case of 'ASEAN' and South Asia", *Gandhi Marg*, Vol. 5, No. 1, April 1983, pp. 45-56.

Pandey, S., ''Mini-maxi Partners: A Look at India - Bhutan Relations'', *Journal of Political Science*, Vol. 48, No. 2, April-June 1982, pp. 86-106.

Pant, Girish, ''Regional Economic Co-operation'', ''Emerging Alliance Between National and International Capital'', *Problems of Non-alignment* (Delhi), Vol. 1, No. 3, September-November 1983.

------, ''Gains from Regional Economic Co-operation'', *Mainstream* (New Delhi), Vol. XXIV, No. 13-14, 30 November, 1985.

Pant, Girish P., and Bista, Nirmal K. ''Thoughts on Trade Models and Trade in South Asia'', *South Asia Forum*, Vol. 1, No. 1, Winter 1981, pp. 15-28.

Parakh, H.T. ''Prospect for Regional Co-operation in South Asia'', *Capital* (Annual No.), 1978-79, pp. 135-7.

Pant, V.P. ''Economics of Regional Co-operation'' *South Asia Forum*, Vol. 1, No. 1, Winter 1981, pp. 43-6.

P.C. Pseud. ''A Worthwhile Move for South Asian Co-operation'', *Radical Humanist*, Vol. 47, No. 12, March, 1984, pp. 4-6.

Phadnis, Umashankar, ''Progress So Far: Some Visible Gains'', *World Focus*, Vol. 3, No. 3, March 1982, pp. 12-14.

------, ''South Asian Co-operation'', *Indian and Foreign Review*, Vol. 19, No. 11, Maexh 15, 1982, pp. 9-10.

Philip Derby, ''Stability Mechanism in South East Asia: Prospects for Regionalism'', *International Affairs*, Vol. 49, No. 1, January 1973, pp. 31.

Pokhral, G.P. ''Regional Co-operation: A Nepalese Viewpoint'', *Indian and Foreign Review*, Vol. 20, No. 20, August 1-14, 1983, pp. 19-21.

Potter, William, C., ''Strategic Consequences of Nuclear Proliferation in South Asia for the Soviet Union'', *Journal of Strategic Studies*, Vol. 8, No. 4, December 1985, pp. 40-48.

Prabhakara, M.S., ''Bangladesh: Fears of Big Brother'' and ''Enormous Goodwill'', *Strategic Digest*, Vol. 14, No. 12, December 1984, pp. 1566-76.

Puchala, Donald, ''International Transactions and Regional Integration'', *International Organisation*, Vol. XXIV, No. 4, Autumn 1970, pp. 732-63.

Quasim, Abul, ''Regional Trade in South Asia: Need to boost Non-traditional Exports'', *Third World*, Vol. 5, No. 5 6, September-October and November-December 1984, pp. 20-23.

Qui Tong Chang and Zhen Hu, "Minister Woos South Asian Nations" *Beijing Review*, Vol. 30, No. 35, August 31, 1987, p. 14.

Qureshi, M.L., "Indian Development Strategy and South Asian Regional Co-operation", *India Quarterly*, Vol. 40, Nos. 3 & 4, July-December 1984, pp. 274-76.

-----, "South Asian Economies During 1970s: The Overall Views", *South Asian Studies* (Islamabad), Vol. 1, No. 1, January 1984, pp. 9-23.

Razvi, Mujtaba, "South Asia and the SAARC", *Pakistan Horizon*, Vol. 39, No. 1, 1986, pp. 120-27.

Robinson, Francis, "Islam and Muslim Society in South Asia", *Contributions to Indian Sociology*, Vol. 17, No. 2, July-December 1983, pp. 185-204.

Roerich, G.N. "The Cultural Unity of Asia", *India Quarterly* (New Delhi), Vol. VI, No. 1, January-March 1950, pp. 38-44.

Ronald, J. Yalem, "Regionalism and World Order", *International Affairs* (London) Vol. 38, No. 4, October, 1962, p. 466.

Rothgeb, John M., "Effects of Foreign Investment on Overall and Sectoral growth in Third World State", *Journal of Peace Research*, Vol. 21, No. 1, 1984, pp. 5-16.

Sabaratnam, T.A., "View from Sri Lanka", *Indian and Foreign Review*, Vol. 20, No. 20, August 1-14, 1983, pp. 24-25.

Saigal, Jagdish C. "Launching Co-operation in South Asia: Main Issues" *Man and Development*, Vol. 4, No. 3, September 1982, pp. 57-65.

Sadani, Zafar, "SAARC–Steady Progress", *Pakistan and Gulf Economist*, Vol. 6, No. 46, November 14, 1987, pp. 8-11.

Sammufathasan, N., "Sri Lanka: The Story of the Holocuast", *Race and Class*, Vol. 26, No. 1, Summer, 1984, pp. 63-82.

Sareen, Rajendra, "South Asian Regional Co-operation", *Indian and Foreign Review*, Vol. 20, No. 20, August 1-14, 1983, pp. 12-15.

Sathe, R.D. "Speech at the Foreign Secretaries of South Asian Countries Meeting, Colombo", April 21, 1981, *Foreign Affairs Record*, Vol. 27, No. 4, April 1981, pp. 126-9.

Satish Kumar, "International Perception", *World Focus*, Vol. 4, 11-12, November-December 1983, pp. 27-30.

-----, "Indian and South Asian Sub-system", *Asian Economist*, Vol. 1, No. 5, 1978, pp. 5-9.

Salaluddin Ahmed, ''Identity of the Subcontinent'', *India International Centre Quarterly*, Vol. 14, No. 2, Summer 1987, pp. 79-88.

Sathyamurthy, T.V. ''Contemporary European Scholarship and Political and Social Change in South Asia: An essay in the sociology of knowledge'', *Economic and Political Weekly*, Vol. 22, No. 1, March 14, 1987, pp. 459-65.

Sawhney, R.G., ''South Asia: Aprop to Pakistan'', *World Focus*, 6(1) January 1985, pp. B-16.

----, ''Zia's Rise to Power'', *Strategic Analysis*, Vol. 8, No. 6, September 1984, pp. 511-24.

-----. ''Pakistan's Military Capability'', *Strategic Analysis*, Vol. 8, No. 7, October 1984, pp. 607-33.

Schmitter, Philip C., ''The Neo-Functional Hypothesis about International Integration'', *International Organisation*, Vol. XXIII, No. 1, Winter, 1969, pp. 161-66.

----, ''Further Notes on Operationalising Some Variables Related to Regional Integration'' *International Organisation*, Vol. XXIII, No. 2, Spring 1969, pp. 327-336.

----, ''A Revised Theory of Regional Integration'', *International Organisation*, Vol. XXIV, Autumn 1970, pp. 840-42.

Seetharam, G.N. ''Limits to South Asian Co-operation'', *Mainstream*, Vol. 22, No. 33, April 14, pp. 11-14, 26.

Segal, Aron, ''The Integration of Developing Countries: Some Thoughts of East-Africa and Central America'', *Journal of Common Market Studies*, Vol.V, No. 3, March 1967, pp. 252-282.

'Seminar' Pakistan Perceptions, *Seminar* No. 303, November 1984, pp.12-48.

Sen Gupta, Bhabani, ''Political Institutions in South Asia'', *World Focus*, Vol. 6, No. 9, September 1985, pp. 19-22.

-----, ''South Asia: Sea of Troubles'', *South*, No. 82, August 1987, pp. 32-33.

Sethi, J.D., ''Summit Lessons for India'', *Indian Express* (Cochin), 6 December, 1985.

Shaha, Rishikesh, ''Imperatives for Regional Co-operation in South Asia'', *South Asia Forum*, Vol. 1, No. 1, Winter 1981, pp. 1-6.

Shamsul Haq, M., ''SAARC: Past, Present and Future'', *Biss Journal*, Vol. 7, No. 3, July 1986, pp. 424-41.

Sharma, Dhirendra, ''Defining the Defence for South Asia'', *Janata*, Vol. 43, No. 9, May 29, 1988, pp. 11-12.

Sharma, L.K., "SAARC Moves Forward," *Indian and Foreign Review*, Vol. 24, No. 4, December 15, 1986, pp. 4-10.

Sharma, K.D., "Regional Co-operation in South Asia: India's Perceptions", *Pakistan and Gulf Economist*, Vol. 3, No. 15, April 14, 1984, pp. 9-13.

Sharma, Satya P., "Materialist Thesis on the Origin and Continuity of the Caste System in South Asia", *Eastern Anthropologist*, Vol. 36, No. 1, January-March 1983, pp. 55-78.

Shelley, Mizamur Rahman, "Bangladesh the Quest for International Recognition", *Asian Affairs*, Vol. 5, No. 4, October-December 1983, pp. 399-419.

Shibusawa, A.H., "Co-operation in Water Resources Development in South Asia: Need for a Fresh Approach", *South Asia Journal*, Vol. 1, No. 3, January-March 1988, pp. 317-28.

Siddiqui, M.A., "SAARC Breaks New Ground", *Pakistan and Gulf Economist*, Vol. 4, No. 21, May 25-31, 1985, pp. 61-62.

Singh, K.R. "Regional Co-operation in South Asia: Security Dimension", *Mainstream*, Vol. 21, No. 31, April 2, 1983, pp. 11-12.

Singh, Natwar, "Interview: SAARC should now have Afghanistan", *Link*, Vol. 30, No. 41, May 15, 1988, pp. 4-6.

South, "A Policy Underprinted by Double-dealing", *South*, No.75, January 1987, pp. 12-13.

Strategic Studies, "South Asian Regional Co-operation", *Strategic Studies*, Vol. 5, No. 4, Summer 1982, pp. 6-8.

Subas, R., "Dynamics of Development in South Asia", *Mainstream*, Vol. 22, No. 49, August 4, 1984, pp. 15-9, 24.

Subramanian, R.R., "U.S. Nuclear Guarantee for Pakistan?", *Strategic Analysis*, Vol. 8, No. 8, November 1984, pp. 707-27.

Subramanyam, K., "India's Security – Present and Future", *Strategic Analysis*, Vol. 8, No. 8, November 1984, pp.716.27.

----, Strategic Perception, *World Focus*, Vol. 4, Nos.11-12, November-December 1983, pp.31-4, fourth annual number 'South Asia Today'.

----, "Strategic Aspect of SARC", *Mainstream*, Vol. XXIV, No. 13 & 14, 30 November 1985.

----, "Nation State Building in South Asia", *Strategic Analysis*, Vol. 8, No.10, January 1985, pp. 907-26.

Suryanaryanan V., "Neighbourhood diplomacy in South Asian Partners in Progression – Uneasy Co-existence: An Indian View", *Asian Studies*, 3 (3-4), July-December 1985, pp. 1-6.

Suhrke, Astri, ''Lessons in Regional Co-operation'', *Indian Express* (Cochin), 9 December 1985.

Sutter, Robert ''Strategic Consequence of Nuclear Proleferation in South Asia for China'', *Journal of Strategic Studies*, Vol. 8, No. 4, December 1985, pp. 49-58.

Singh, Tarlok, ''Studies for Co-operation and Development in South Asia'', *India Quarterly*, Vol. 34, No.4, October-December 1978, pp. 516-19.

----, ''Social Science Research and South Asian Co-operation'', *South Asian Journal*, Vol. 1, No. 1, July-September 1987, pp. 81-87.

---, ''Expansion of Trade between India and SARC Countries'', *Monthly Commentary on Indian Economic Conditions*, Vol. 27, No. 1, August 1985, pp. 47-50.

---, ''Development Planning in South Asia and the Current Challenges'', *Indian Journal of Public Administration*, Vol. 30, No. 3, July-September 1984, pp. 497-507.

----, ''Economic Development and Co-operation in South Asia: A Design for Co-operative Study'', *Third World Quaterly*, Vol. 1, No. 1, January 1979, pp. 117-23.

----, ''Directions of Advances in SARC'', *Mainstream* (New Delhi) , Vol. XXIV, No. 13 & 14, 30 November 1985.

----, ''Economic Co-operation in South Asia'', *Indian and Foreign Review*, Vol. 19, No. 17, June 15, 1982, pp. 13-14.

Sobhan, Rehman, ''Political Economy of South Asian Co-operation'', *South Asia Journal*, Vol. 1, No. 3, January-March, 1988, pp. 237-52.

'Spotlight on Regional Affairs', ''SAARC: The Urge for Co-operation in South Asia'', *Spotlight on Regional Affairs*, Vol. 5, No. 2, February 1986.

Sreedhar, ''India's Neighbours: Quest for Security in the Absence of Legitimacy'', *Strategic Analysis*, Vol. 7, No. 12, March 1984, pp. 1012-20.

----, ''Prospects for SARC: A Novel Venture'', *Strategic Analysis*, Vol. 19, No.1, April 1985, pp. 11-14.

----, ''South Asian Security Perspectives'', *Strategic Analysis*, Vol. 7, No. 10, January 1984, pp. 767-79.

Sri Lanka, *Strategic Digest*, Vol. 14, No. 12, December 1984, pp. 1444-65.

Srivastava, R.K., and Kothari, Rajini, 'SAARC', *Seminar*, No. 324, August 1986, pp. 22-26.

Tellis, Ashley, J., "Naval Balance in the Indian Sub-continent", *Asian Survey*, Vol. 25, No. 12, December 1985, pp. 1186-1213.

Thomas, Raju G.C., "Security Relationship in Southern Asia", *Asian Survey*, Vol. 21, No.7, July 1981, pp. 698-709.

Tornquist, Olle, "Class and Democracy in South and South-East Asia: Some Critical Notes", *Co-operation and Conflict*, 1985, pp. 113-26.

Vaidyanathan, C.V. "SARC Enters Crucial Phase", Vol. 2, No. 20, August 15, 1984, pp. 15-28.

Vishal, Singh, "Regional Co-operation in Southern Asia: A Proposal", *Asian Studies*, No. 5, February 1983, pp. 1-7.

Vanaik, Achin, "Political Case for NWFZ in South Asia," *Economic and Political Weekly*, Vol. 20, No. 48, November 30, 1985, pp. 2115-20.

Varshney, R.I., and Raj Kumar, "SAARC will bring Peace in the South Asian Region", *Commerce*, Vol. 156, No. 4007, March 5, 1988, pp.24-7.

Vasudevan, Parvathi, "India and Her Neighbours" *IDSA Journal*, Vol. 16, No. 1, July-September 1983, pp. 33-39.

Venkatasubbiah, H., "Prospects for an Asian Union: Lessons from the Organization of American States", *India Quarterly*, Vol. 5, No.2, April-June 1949, pp. 99-112.

Virsingh, Suneet, "Mutual Image Perceptions in South Asia", *Mainstream* (New Delhi), Vol. XXIV, No. 13-14, 30 November 1985.

Viswam, S., "SAARC: Potential for Regional Benefits", *Democratic World*, 14(50), December 15, 1985, pp. 56.

-----, "Lots of hope in SAARC", *World Focus*, Vol. 17, Nos. 11-12, November-December 1986, pp. 42-44, 47.

Udyashankar, B., "Limits and Limitations of SAARC", *Strategic Analysis*, Vol. 9, No.11, February 1986, pp. 1059-68.

----, "Recent Major Development in South Asia" *Strategic Analysis*, Vol. 9, No. 5, August 1985, pp. 431-39.

Usman, S.M., "Delhi Declarations on Regional Co-operation", *Pakistan and Gulf Economist*, Vol. II, No. 21, May 21-27, 1983, pp. 8-13.

Vaitsos, Costantine, "Crisis in Regional Economic Co-operation (Integration) Among Developing Countries: A Survey", *World Development*, Vol. 6 (1978), pp. 719-69.

Waquif, Arif A., "Exploiting Potential Areas of Industrial Co-operation in South Asia", *South Asia Journal*, Vol. 1, No. 1, July-September 1987, pp. 51-63.

Wells, Raymonds J.G., "Inter-regional Co-operation in Asean", *Asia Pacific Community*, No. 24, Spring 1984, pp. 85-93.

Wink, Andre, "Sovereignty and Universal Dominion in South Asia", No. 3, July-September 1984, pp. 265-92.

Wrising, Robert G., "Dilemmas in the U.S.-Pakistan Security Relationship", *Asian Affairs*, Vol. II, No. 2, Summer 1984, pp. 12-39.

——, "Arms Race in South Asia: Implication for the U.S.". *Asian Survey*, Vol. 25, No. 3, March 1985, pp. 265-91.

Wriggins, Howard, "Pakistan's Search for a Foreign Policy After the Invasion of Afghanistan", *Pacific Affairs*, Vol. 57, Summer 1984, pp. 284-303.

Wright, Denis, "Diplomatic Relations Between the States of the Indian Sub-continent", *World Review*, Vol. 22, No. 4. October 1983, pp. 70-80.

Ziring, Lawrence, "From Islamic Republic to Islamic State in Pakistan", *Asian Survey*, Vol. 24, No. 9, September, 1984, pp. 931-46.

——, United States and Pakistan: Troubled Alliance", *Asian Affairs*, Vol. 5, No. 2, April-July 1983, pp. 156-71.

——, "Political Dilemmas and Instability in South and South-West Asia", *Asian Affairs*, Spring 1983, pp. 37-47.

Index

d. mobilization of regional external resources;

e. identification of new areas of co-operation based on appropriate studies.

2. The Standing Committee shall meet as often as deemed necessity.

3. The Standing Committee shall submit periodic reports to the Council of Ministers and make reference to it as and when necessary for decision of policy matters.

Article VI

Technical Committees

1. Technical Committees comprising representatives of Member States shall be responsible for the implementation, co-ordination and monitoring of the programmes in their respective areas of co-operation.

2. They shall have the following terms of reference :

a. determination of the potential and the scope of regional co-operation in agreed areas;

b. formulation of programmes and preparation of projects;

c. determination of financial implications of sectoral programmes;

d. formulation of recommendations regarding apportionment of costs;

e. implementation and co-ordination of sectoral programmes;

f. monitoring of progress in implementation.

3. the Technical Committees shall submit periodic reports to the Standing Committee.

4. The Chairmanship of the Technical Committees shall normally rotate among Member States in alphabetical order on every two years.

5. The Technical Committees may, *inter alia*, use the following mechanism and modalities, if and when considered necessary:

a. meeting of heads of national technical agencies;

b. meetings of experts in specific fields;

c. contact amongst recognized centres of excellence in the region.

Article VII

Action Committees

The Standing Committee may set up Action Committees comprising

Member States concerned with implementation of projects involving more than two but not all Member States.

Article VIII

Secretariat

There shall be Secretariat of the ASSOCIATION

Article IX

Financial Arrangements

1. The contribution of each Member State towards financing of the activities of the ASSOCIATION shall be voluntary.

2. Each Technical Committee shall make recommendations for the apportionment of costs of implementing the programmes proposed by it.

3. In case sufficient financial resources cannot be mobilized within the region for funding activities of the ASSOCIATION, external financing from appropriate sources may be mobilized with the approval of or by the Standing Committee.

Article X

General Provisions

1. Decisions at all levels shall be taken on the basis of unanimity.

2. Bilateral and contentious issues shall be excluded from the deliberations.

IN FAITH WHEREOF we have set our Hands And Seals Hereunto DONE IN DHAKA, BANGLADESH. On This The Eighth Day of December Of The Year One Thousand Nine Hundred Eighty Five.

Hussain Muhammed Ershad
PRESIDENT OF THE
PEOPLES REPUBLIC OF
BANGLADESH

Birendra Bir
Bikram Shah Dev
KING OF NEPAL

Maumoon Abdul Gayoom
PRESIDENT OF THE
REPUBIC OF
MALDIVES

Rajiv Gandhi
PRIME MINISTER
OF THE REPUBLIC
OF INDIA

Jigme Singye Wangchuck
KING OF BHUTAN

Muhammed Zia-ul-Haq
PRESIDENT OF THE
ISLAMIC REPUBLIC
OF PAKISTAN

Junius Richard Jayawardene

PRESIDENT OF DEMOCRATIC
SOCIALIST REPUBLIC OF SRILANKA

BIBLIOGRAPHY

Primary Sources

New Delhi, Ministry of External Affairs, Report of the Technical Committees on Agriculture, Dhaka, 9-11 October, 1983 (SARC/Sc/1).

------ , Ministry of External Affairs, Report of the Technical Committee on Postal Services, Thimpu, 27-29 October, 1983 (SARC/Sc/4).

------ , Ministry of External Affairs, Report of the Technical Committee of Scientific and Technological Co-operation, Islamabad, 21-23 December, 1983 (SARC/Sc/6).

------ , Ministry of External Affairs, Report of the Technical Committee on Telecommunications, Islamabad, 21-22 November, 1983 (SARC/Sc/8).

------ , Ministry of External Affairs, Report of the Technical Committee on Transport, Male, 15-17 October, 1983 (SARC/Sc/9).

------, Ministry of External Affairs, Report of the Technical Committee on Health and Population Activities, Kathmandu, 15-17 January, 1984 (SARC/Sc/2).

------ , Ministry of External Affairs, Report of the Technical Committee on Meteorology, New Delhi, 3-7 January, 1984 (SARC/Sc/3).

------ , Ministry of External Affairs, Report of the Technical Committee, on Rural Development, Colombo, 16-17 January, 1984 (SARC/Sc/5).

------ , Ministry of External Affairs, Report of the Technical Committee on Sports, Arts and Culture, 13-14 January, 1984 (SARC/Sc/7).

Joint Communique: First meeting of South Asian Foreign Secretaries, Colombo, 23 April, 1981.

New Delhi, External Publicity Division, Ministry of External Affairs, Six-nation summit on Nuclear disarmament: Delhi Declaration, 20 January, 1985.

Sri Lanka Ministry of Foreign Affairs Press Release No. 79/80.

''Dhaka Declaration'', *Commerce*, Vol. 151, No. 3891, December 21, 1985, pp. 1102-3.

Documents, SARC, *India Quarterly*, Vol. 40, Nos. 3 & 4, July-December 1984, pp. 323-396.

Gandhi, Indira, Inaugural Address at the Meeting of the South Asian Foreign Ministers, Vol. 29, No. 33, August 13-19, 1983.

Meeting of Foreign Secretaries of South Asian Countries, 1st, April 20-22 1981, Colombo, Joint Communique, Colombo, April 22, 1981, *Asian Recorder*, Vol. 27, No. 28, July 9-15, 1981.

Meeting of the Foreign Secretaries of South Asian Countries, 3rd, August 7-9, 1982, Islamabad, Joint Communique, Islamabad, August 9, 1982, *Pakistan Horizon*, Vol. 35, No.3, 1982, pp. 137-9.

Meeting of Foreign Ministers of Seven South Asian Countries, 2nd, July 10-11, Male, Joint Communique, Male, July 11, 1984, *Asian Recorder*, Vol. 30, No. 37, September 9-15, 1984.

Meeting of Foreign Ministers of Seven South Asian Countries, 1st, August 1-2, 1983, New Delhi, "Declaration on South Asian Regional Co-operation", New Delhi, August 2, 1983, *Asian Recorder*, Vol. 29, No. 33, August 13-19, 1983.

Meeting of Foreign Secretaries of South Asian Countries, 4th, Dhaka, Joint Communique, Dhaka, March 29, 1983, *Asian Recorder*, Vol. 29, No. 20, May 14-20, 1983, p. 17160.

Narasimha Rao, P.V., Address to the South Asian Regional Co-operation Standing Committee, New Delhi, February 27, 1984, *Foreign Affairs Record*, Vol. 30, No. 2, February 1984, pp. 71-74.

Pakistan and South Asia: Declaration on South Asian Regional Co-operation, *Pakistan Horizon*, Vol. 36, No. 3, 1983, pp. 184-1847.

SAARC: India -- A Partner in Co-operation, External Publicity Division, Ministry of External Affairs, New Delhi.

"SAARC Charter", *Commerce*, Vol. 151, No. 3891, December 21, 1985, pp. 1103-4.

South Asia Regional Co-operation Programme, press release (Text), New Delhi, January 10, 1984, *Foreign 'Affairs Record* Vol. 30, No. 1, January 1984, p. 27.

South Asia Regional Co-operation, Standing Committee (SARC), Session, 1st, February 27-29, 1984, New Dehi (Chairman: M. Rasgotra), Report (Extr.), *Indian and Foreign Review*, Vol. 21, No. 11, March 31, 1984, pp. 8-9, 11.

South Asia Regional Co-operation, Standing Committee (Chairman: M. Rasgotra), Press release on the report at the conclusion of the First session (Text), New Delhi, Feb. 28, 1984, *Foreign Affairs Record*, Vol. 30, No. 2, February 1984, pp. 76-8.

Documents, Third SAARC Summit, Kathmandu, 1987, *South Asia Journal*, Vol. 1, No. 3, January-March 1988, pp. 329-50.

Sri Lanka Foreign Affairs Record 1985-1986.

Yaqub Khan, Sahabzada, ''Inaugural address at the Meeting of Foreign Secretaries of the South Asian Region, Islamabad'', August, 1982, pp. 135-4, pp. 135-47.

Secondary Sources: Books

Agwani, M.S. *et al* ed., *South Asia: Stability and Regional Co-operation*, (Chandigarh, 1983).

Aiyar, S.P., *Commonwealth in South Asia* (New Delhi, 1969).

Ajit Singh Sarhadi, *India's Security in Resurgent Asia* (New Delhi, 1979).

Almond, Gabriel and Colman J., eds., *The Politics of the Developing Areas* (Princeton, 1960).

Alger, Chadwick R., ''Comparison of International and International Politics'', in R. Barry Farrall ed., *Approaches to Comparative and International Politics* (Evanston, 1966), pp. 301-328.

Andic, Fuat, *et al.*, *A Theory of Economic Integration For Development Countries* (London, 1971).

Appadorai, A. and Rajan M.S., *India's Foreign Policy and Relations* (New Delhi, 1985).

Axline, Andrew W., *Carribean Integration, The Politics of Regionalism* (London, 1979).

Ayoob, Muhammed, *India, Pakistan and Bangladesh: Search for a New Relationship* (New Delhi, 1975).

Brodie, Henry, *et al.*, *South Asia in the World Today* (Chicago, 1950).

Badgley, John, *Asian Development: Problems and Prognosis* (New York, 1971).

Beer, F.A.: *Alliances: Latent War Communities in the Contemporary World* (New York, 1971).

Brecher, Micheal, *The New States of Asia: A Political Analysis* (London, 1963).

Behrman, Jack, *Problems of Regional Integration in Latin America* (New York, 1968).

Barnada, William J., *India, Pakistan, and the Great Powers* (New York, 1972).

Balassa, Bela, *The Theory of Economic Integration* (Homewood, 1961).

Bajpai, U.S. ed., *India and its Neighbourhood* (New Delhi, 1986).

Caparaso, James A., *The Structure and Function of European Integration* (Pacific Palisades, 1974).

Chufan, G., *Economic Co-operation and Collective Security in Asia* (New Delhi, 1976).

Cochrane, J., *Politics of Regional Integration: The Central American Case* (New Orleans, 1969).

Claude Jr. Inis, *Swords into Ploughshares* (New York, 1956).

Clark, W.H., *The Politics of the Common Market* (Englewood Cliffs, N.J., 1967).

Chopra, Pran *et al*, *Future of South Asia* (Delhi, 1986).

Cruden, Robert, *et al*, ed., *New Perspectives on America and South Asia* (New Delhi, 1984).

David Mytrany, *A Working Peace System* (London, 1946).

David Singer ed., *Quantitative International Politics: Insights and Evidence* (New York, 1967).

Department of State Publication 7410, *The Sub-continent of South Asia* (Washington 25, D.C., 1962).

Deutsch, K., *Political Community at the International Level* (Princeton, 1954).

Deutsch, K., *et al.*, *Political Communities and North Atlantic Area* (Princeton, 1957).

Dutt, V.P., *India's Foreign Policy* (New Delhi, 1984).

Etzioni, Amitai, *Political Unification: A Comparative Study of Leaders and Forces* (New York, 1965).

George, Timothy, *India and the Great Powers* (Aldershot, International Institute for Strategic Studies 1984).

Gough, Kathleen, and Shaluna P. Hari, eds., *Imperialism and Revolution in South Asia* (New York, 1973).

Galtung, John, *The European Community: A Super Power in the Making* (Oslo, 1973).

Groom, A.J.R. and Paul Taylor eds., *Functionalism: Theory and Practice in International Relations* (London, 1975).

Gupta, Bhabani Sen, ed., *Regional Co-operation and Development*, Vol. I & II (New Delhi, 1986).

Gupta, Sisir, *India and Regional Integration in Asia* (Bombay, 1964).

Hass, Ernst B., *The Uniting of Europe: Political Forces, 1951-1957* (Standard, Calif, 1968).

------ , *The Obsolescence of Regional Integration Theory* (Berkely, 1975).

------ , *Beyond the Nation State* (Stanford, 1964).

Hayter, Teresa, *Aid as Imperialism* (Middlesex, 1971).

Indorf, Hans H., *Impediments to Regionalism in South East Asia: Bilateral Constraints Among ASEAN Member States* (Singapore, 1984).

Jackson, Robert, *South Asian Crisis: India, Pakistan and Bangladesh* (London, 1975).

Kahnert, F. *et al.*, *Economic Integration Among Developing Countries* (Paris, 1969).

Kaplan Mortan A., System and Process in International Affairs (New York, 1964).

Kitamura, Hiroshi, ''Economic Theory and the Economic Integration of underdeveloped Regions'', in M. Wionczek ed., *Latin American Economic Integration: Experiences and Prospects* pp. 42-63 (New York, 1966).

Lawrence, Ziring, ed., *The Sub-continent in World Politics* (New York, 1978).

Levi, Werner, *The Challenge of World Politics in South and South East Asia* (Englewood Cliffs, N.J., 1968).

Lloyed I. Rudolph and Suasanne, H.R., eds., *The Regional Imperative* (New Delhi, 1980).

Lindberg, Leon, *The Political Dynamcis of European Integration* (Stanford, 1963).

Lindberg, Leon and Sheingold, *Europe's Would-be Polity* (Englewood Cliffs, N.J., 1970).

Lindberg, Leon and Sheingold, Stuart A., *Regional Integration: Theory and Research* (Hardward, 1971).

Machlup, Fritz, *Economic Integration Worldwide, Regional, Sectoral* (London, 1976).

M.C. Cowan, Patrick J. and Howard Shapiro, *The Comparative Study of Foreign Policy* (Beverly Hills, 1973).

Milenky, Edward S., *The Politics of Regional Organisation in Latin America* (New York, 1973).